How to achieve the unthinkable, earn more money,
and create the success you always desired.

UNSTOPPABLE
SUCCESS

Big Sky Publishing Pty Ltd
PO Box 303, Newport, NSW 2106, Australia
Phone: 1300 364 611
Fax: (61 2) 9918 2396
Email: info@bigskypublishing.com.au
Web: www.bigskypublishing.com.au

Cover design and typesetting: Think Productions

 A catalogue record for this
book is available from the
National Library of Australia

Title: Unstoppable Success. How to achieve the unthinkable, earn more money, and create the success you always desired.
ISBN: 978-1-923144170
Author: Jessica Williamson

How to achieve the unthinkable, earn more money,
and create the success you always desired.

UNSTOPPABLE
SUCCESS

BIG SKY PUBLISHING
www.bigskypublishing.com.au

JESSICA WILLIAMSON

Testimonials

'A must-read if you want to level up in business and life. Jess injects her infectious energy and make-anything-happen optimism into every page of this book, which is packed with actionable tips, hard-won advice and proven strategies.'
Lisa Messenger

'Jess doesn't hold back and will have you believing absolutely anything is possible! Jess is the kind of person who makes things happen and is a force to be reckoned with. She shares her unique perspectives and daring stories of creating major success against all odds. There are a tonne of tangible strategies and mindset tools to unlock the power you already have within you and skyrocket toward your goals, regardless of how illogical they may seem, Jess proves you really can have it all and more.'
Sarah Davidson

'Jess's practical advice about making your dreams a reality is perfect for anyone getting started in business and for seasoned entrepreneurs too.'
Kerrie Hess

'This book is so powerful no matter where you are on your entrepreneurial journey. Jess was always a step ahead of everyone else with the businesses she has built. I love her forward-thinking. Jess is the person who's willing to take the risk and put herself out there to experience the hard lessons and then share it with others to learn from her journey.'
Heidi Anderson

'The most important part to me is not even the tangible things I've achieved with Jess' help. It's the emotional support that means the most to me. I can't put a price on that feeling of support that I've never had before, I feel like I'm not doing this all on my own. She's like a secret weapon I can whip out at any time!
"Jess always knows what to do in every business situation. You can save time getting advice from someone who has been there and done that rather than trying to figure it all out yourself.'
Ezereve, Musician & Agency Owner

'I've never experienced a mentor like Jess. She truly cares about you and gets you. Jess pushes you, challenges you and keeps you accountable so you don't get lost she's watching and giving feedback to help me succeed. I've never had so much support.'
Kristy Borbas, Intuitive Mentor & Healer

'Jess helped me create a business that my lifestyle fits into. Jess' support and encouragement gave me the extra confidence to believe in myself to take that leap into my business full time and I've never looked back. After 3 short months of working together, I had x3 my income! Something that I NEVER thought would be possible in my first year of business. Her knowledge is spectacular.'
Samantha, Silk Digital (marketing agency)

'The amount of growth I have had in the last 3 months blows my mind. I'm so grateful to be a part of such a powerful group of women and be coached by someone like Jess'
Shavojn Read, Mindset Mentor

'Jess is truly able to see the blind spots I have in my business and the limiting beliefs that are holding me back from the results I'm craving. Together we worked through my self-worth, values, money mindset and so much more. I doubled my top revenue month in a way that felt so much easier than it ever has before! When Jess talks about her strategy of Building a Business for Life, she means it. My business is taking off, and I can't wait to see what's next for me!
Amanda Riffee, Leadership Coach & Trainer

'Jess, the way you explained the concept of self was unlike I've heard from anyone, and it really hit home! Pinpointing 5 ways I would describe myself and coming to the realisation that my brain is constantly looking for ways or situations to confirm that. With that awareness, I am now choosing to see myself as a successful, powerful entrepreneur and those old people-pleasing ways are a thing of the distant past!'
Vanessa Correa, Marketing

'Jess has expanded my mindset way beyond anything I could have even comprehended. She is the ultimate wing woman in biz & mindset. It's great to have someone there through the tough times in biz, you're not going through it alone. My biz and mindset are accelerating with the help of Jess.'
Vanessa, Organised Style Living

'Jess has completely transformed my business and myself as an entrepreneur, and I'm so grateful. Jess has helped us with figuring out what path is right for what I want to accomplish and what steps I need to take next. Jess has taken our business to the next level in such a short amount of time that I couldn't have accomplished on my own.'
Isabella, Activewear Designer

'I have gained so much confidence within myself and in my thoughts around my pricing offers. Jess has opened my eyes to what is possible when you believe in yourself and keep a positive mindset.'
Candice, Design by Jones (interior design)

'Jess helped me find alignment in what I wanted to do, and she supported me through many huge life changes in my personal life as well. The sales and results we saw while working together were also fantastic, however the feeling of feeling like myself again is priceless.'
Rach Yeung, Marketing Expert

Dedication

To my incredible parents, Sherryl and Wayne, for showing
me what perseverance looks like, always being my biggest
cheerleaders and picking me up when I hit rock bottom.

To my fiancé, Chris, for always seeing the potential and
power in me — even when my ideas were absolutely crazy!

And to YOU!

I wouldn't be writing this book if it wasn't for you and all
the incredible powerhouse women I have had the privilege
to meet and connect with throughout this wild journey so
far. I see you and appreciate you so much.

Contents

Foreword
Lisa Messenger

When it comes to business, there's probably no lesson I haven't learnt, no mistake I haven't made and no path I haven't trodden in my mission to ignite human potential. That's my entire reason for being, my passion: to challenge individuals and corporations to change the way they think, to take them out of their comfort zone and to prove that there is more than one way to do anything.

I'm always thrilled to hear from entrepreneurs and business owners who have read one of my books and it's inspired them on their journey, and Jess is no exception. We first connected a number of years ago in Sydney, when Jess made contact and asked why I hadn't brought my roadshow to her hometown of Perth, Western Australia. I thought, *Well, why haven't I?* Before long, Jess and I had worked together on bringing the event to the West Coast, and it was a full house! I was so inspired by her determination, her innovative spirit, and her willingness to challenge the status quo. She left a real impression on me in our short time together and I knew she was destined for big things!

My philosophy in business and life is always rooted in my deep desire to inspire and motivate others to step into their

1

entrepreneurial spirit, creativity, and innovation. Everything I do and share is to encourage others to live life to the absolute max, in a place where the 'normal' rules don't apply and were doing things 'the way they've always been done' simply doesn't cut it!

Jess has the same philosophy, and it's seen her chart a path of growth and success not only for herself but also for the people she serves as a coach. When I see the results that a small spark of inspiration from one of my books can create in someone like Jess, I'm truly blown away to see just what impact we can make; when one person inspires another, and another, that ripple effect continues and that's how we change the world.

After reading this book, I hope you, too, are ready to step out of your comfort zone, change how you think and step into your true potential to make your mark!

Lisa Messenger
Entrepreneur, founder, and CEO of Collective Hub

> **I've discovered there are no rules in business or life and that YOU get to decide what will be true for you.**

Introduction

I've never been a big reader (she says as she sits here, writing a book for you to read!).

I was the kid in school who chose *Where's Wally* while the others were diving into novels and story books. That is until I found a book that spoke to my soul. It was a business book by a truly inspirational female founder, and I couldn't put it down. It was the first book I ever finished in its entirety. It was 2012 and I read it during my morning train commute to my full-time job, at the ripe old age of 19. Yes, the first book I ever finished was when I was 19!

Daring and Disruptive, by Lisa Messenger, lit a fire under me that sparked my obsession with the possibilities of building my own empire. At the time, I was burnt out and hated the job I was in. I knew I was capable of so much more and was destined for big things, but I didn't know what that looked like.

Fast forward ten years and I'm writing a book about success in business for you. In this book I'm putting it all out there – the good, the bad and the ugly – because my mission is to *really* show you what is possible. I want to do more than just inspire you; I want to prompt you into the boldest action you can take towards your goals. I am here to make a deep impact on women across the globe. I haven't always been confident. In the past, I was the biggest introvert, despite knowing my capabilities, I preferred to remain unnoticed. But I always knew my purpose was bigger than my fear and I consistently pushed myself out of my comfort zone, time and time again. It was scary at times ... but I always believed I was meant for more. And so are you.

I've discovered is that there are no rules in business or life and that YOU get to decide what gets to be true for you. My journey has been by no means linear. I've been through and overcome challenges and roadblocks, and I've learnt more than enough lessons through trial and error. In these pages, I'm going to help you achieve your business goals and show you how to level up your success. I want you to learn the lessons I have learnt along the way and avoid making the mistakes I made.

I will show you how to:

- Develop an unshakeable self-belief and manage your mindset.
- Define what success looks like for you and be clear about what it is you want.
- Harness your thinking and awareness so that you stop getting in your way.
- Think big, believe big and dream big.
- Stop thinking it's all about the money and start feeling wealthy NOW.
- Keep up the momentum once you've levelled up your business success.
- Embrace your failures and love your mistakes.
- Reach your potential in a way you never thought you could.

I hope this book lights a fire inside you, like Lisa's book did for me. I hope this is the spark you need that blows your mind and sets you on the path of finding out what you're *truly* capable of.

Unstoppable Success Workbook

Stop! Don't go any further without downloading your complimentary workbook. It's loaded with essential exercises, reflection and journal prompts to capture the pivotal steps toward building YOUR unstoppable success plan.

So, do the work and dream big – cultivate your badass entrepreneur energy!

Every time you revisit your workbook, you will take away a new outlook on cracking the next level. And then you can dream even bigger, bolder and crazier!

Scan the QR code or head to jessicawilliamson.com.au/workbook to download.

Holy shit – what am I going to do?

The Tipping Point

Back in 2016 when I was 22-year-old Jess in Perth, Western Australia, I was working in a junior marketing job and preparing to launch my own fashion business – despite the fact I had no experience running a business or manufacturing a product, no credentials or contacts, no partners or investors, no money behind me and no inheritance or family money to tap into.

It was about mid-way through 2016, I was working my full-time job in marketing, which paid $40,000 per year, while putting at least 50 hours a week into my first business, a swimwear label. I'd wake up early to try and get on top of my admin and pack orders for my business before leaving for work at 7 am, then on my lunch breaks, I'd race to the post office to send packages and reconcile invoices. When I'd finally get home after 6 pm I would open my laptop and dive into the business once again ... I never stopped.

The hours were clearly not sustainable long term – no one can work 90 to 100 hours a week without an impact on their health and wellbeing. It was *a lot*. To say I was running myself into the ground was an understatement. I was burnt out to the max.

If you think it couldn't get worse, it did. Around six months into my business journey, I learned that getting a business off the ground costs a lot of money upfront.

One morning, after I had parked my car I swiped my debit card to pay the $12 daily fee for parking, my card was declined. I tried again – *declined*.

I logged into my internet banking and when I saw the balance – $2.20, I felt like I'd been punched in the gut. ***What?! How is this possible?***

When I started work I focused on having a safety savings buffer. From that time, I aimed to always have a minimum of $10,000 in my account … until that moment. With my heart thumping in my chest and panic rising in my throat I stared at my phone, completely shocked, trying to make sense of the situation.

My ENTIRE life savings were gone. How?

Yes, I had started a product-based business on my own and shelled out thousands of dollars in upfront expenses. And, yes, I was quickly learning – at the beginning of fast scaling a business money flows *out* faster than it flows in.

But I hadn't realised I was at the stage of having **NEGATIVE** dollars to my name.

I broke down and cried. Like, really ugly cried out in front of the office. People were staring at me with the strangest looks as I stood there, frozen, trying to figure out what to do next.

I felt stuck. Stuck in the job I hated, stuck with my health suffering, stuck feeling burnt out and stuck daydreaming about my big bold goals of creating my dream business but feeling those goals were now almost over before they had even begun.

Seeing negative dollars in my account was the last straw. It felt like my whole world had come crashing down. All the hard work I had put in – the early mornings, the late nights, the missed social gatherings, the sacrifices and challenges – were they all for nothing?

Holy shit – what am I going to do? Do I just give up and go home?

That was my first thought – to escape. Home was an hour away; I was already late for work and I didn't actually have any cash at home to pay for this $12 parking fee.

Do I borrow money?

Common sense kicked in and I realised I was going to have to borrow the cash. The tricky part – if I rushed inside to borrow money from a work friend, I'd risk a $60 fine.

Do I just keep crying?

Yep, sounds like a plan. After another 15 minutes of ugly crying and feeling sorry for myself, I finally pulled myself together.

I sprinted into the office and found my closest work friend. I lied and told her that mysteriously, both the parking machine *and* my phone weren't working (oh, ego – I had so much to learn about the power of vulnerability and honesty!).

Thankfully, she gave me the money without questioning my rather far-fetched story and I sorted the parking issue. Then as I ran back to my desk and sat down to log into my emails, my stomach rumbled.

Shit.

I hadn't eaten breakfast that morning because I was in such a rush trying to juggle my business and my work that I'd raced out the door without eating. Because I had been 'so busy', I didn't make myself any lunch and figured I would have to just buy it that day … with money I now realised I didn't have.

I had no money, no food, and what felt like no options. I was on the verge of a full-scale breakdown. And in that moment, I knew something had to change. Something BIG.

I could have said to myself:

- You know what? Business is just not for me.
- I don't ever want to feel this again.
- I'm never taking a risk again.
- I'm not capable of this.
- I am not good with money.
- Business causes me insane stress and anxiety.
- When I chase my dreams, bad things happen.

Any of these statements would have been reasonable. I mean, the evidence was right there! Right?

I'm not saying that this is going to be easy,
it's not always going to be a walk in the
park. But what's on the other side is the
life and business of your wildest dreams,
and it's undeniably worth it.

I had so much self-belief that some
people honestly thought I was delusional
(all the best people are!).

CHAPTER 1

A Big Dreamer with a Sprinkle of Delusion

I've always been a big dreamer with a sprinkle of delusion.

No, really ... Picture me, second-grade Jess, with whiter-than-white blonde hair neatly tied in two plaits, in my cute school uniform – with a badass vision for what would become my first-ever business experience, the 'Girls Club'. I offered paid memberships for planned lunchtime activities. It was a hit. As my members grew so did my plans. Until I hit my first roadblock, and it was a big one! When the teachers heard I was taking money from other students they insisted that I refund the money and shut down the club.

But I wasn't put off. Not in the slightest.

My tenacity, my big dreams and what some might call my delusional mindset weren't going to be dimmed by something as small as a teacher telling me no. When I was 17, I chose my university degree based purely on the fact that I knew I was going to be a badass CEO. As you're about to learn in this book, I went on to create a life of wild levels of success, wealth, and growth. But seriously, there are *so many reasons* why I shouldn't be this successful. I didn't follow a traditional path and I didn't wait until I had all the experience, the education, and the expertise under my belt to go out and take the crazy leaps I did; it wasn't too long ago that it seemed like my badass CEO, Unstoppable Success entrepreneur dreams were not destined to happen for me.

Hitting Rock Bottom

When 22-year-old Jess was standing at the parking garage ugly sobbing over a negative bank balance it honestly could have been hands up, waving the white flag moment, but I knew it couldn't be.

Someone on the outside looking in would probably have thought there were 108,000 different reasons why I shouldn't have been able to scale this mountain and achieve what I did. But regardless of how hard things became I had absolute self-belief down to my core that I could create FANTASY LAND levels of success.

> **Somehow, it never crossed my mind to give up. All I could see was expansion, despite all the scarcity surrounding me. THIS was, and is, my biggest superpower.**

I knew that Badass CEO Jess just needed to believe in herself. So, I took a breath and said to myself:

- You know what? Business is for me.
- If you feel this way again, harness the energy, and the lessons, and make it happen against all odds.
- I'm not afraid of taking a risk.
- I'm capable of this.

- I am good with money.
- Business does not cause me insane stress and anxiety.
- When I chase my dreams, I make things happen.

When I look back, I can see how powerful that was and I'm so grateful that my mind worked in that way – with rock-solid belief and absolutely no doubt that I was going to create success.

Even though I was at rock bottom, burnt out (to the max) and my health was being completely neglected, all I could see was a way forward. The reality is no one stole money out of my bank account. I just had no budget whatsoever, so I learnt a big lesson. I'd spent all my hard-earned savings on building my business, but I didn't pay attention to the money coming in and out.

The reason I spent all that money, however, is because I had absolute self-belief that my goals were not just possible, but INEVITABLE. Investing in myself and my goals over the years has been the best thing I have ever done for my growth and success because in times like these, it allows you to dig yourself out of the trenches and see the bigger picture. I had so much self-belief that some people honestly thought I was delusional (all the best people are). My logical brain jumped in and said, 'What's next?'

Self-belief helped me through the toughest moments because I knew success was just around the corner – even when I hit rock bottom.

At that moment, I called my mum (who else do you call when you're 22 and an emotional wreck?). She answered the phone and just said, 'Don't worry, Jess, I'll bring you some coins.' She dropped whatever she was doing and drove an hour to bring me money and reassurance.

When Mum arrived and crossed the road to my office, I was standing outside crying. She hugged me and handed me one of those small zip-lock plastic bags with a few coins in to pay my friend back, and she'd also brought me a packed lunch from home so that I could survive another day. I am beyond grateful for the support from my family, especially my mum, in those early days. Having people who truly support you, even when you probably look absolutely crazy, is everything.

I picked myself up and continued with my business as if nothing had happened: promoting, marketing, showing up on social media and working towards my goals. And because of my determination and ability to keep on moving, I went on to turn over $300,000 in that first year. This was my first year ever running a business, in a highly competitive industry, where most consumers purchase a new swimsuit once a year, body image plays a role in purchase behaviour, and the brand was completely online so people couldn't try anything on before buying – all major factors of resistance.

Unshakeable self-belief means you have so much trust in your ability to make it work, that you can take the leap, even when you don't know how it will work out.

This is the power of unshakeable self-belief. I could see the roadblocks in front of me, but I wasn't prepared to let anything stop me – and instead, I moved forward as if my goals were inevitable.

Rewriting my Story

Those were certainly stressful days at the beginning. But since then, I have built five successful businesses and become a thought leader, TEDx Speaker and Business and Mindset Mentor. I didn't let that one moment in time define me and I didn't let it become the story about who I was and who I could be. I had absolute belief that I was capable of so much more. I picked myself up. I had a bit of a cry. And I kept going.

From rock bottom, you can rewrite your story and make it anything you want to be. It's up to you to decide what you focus on — the opportunities or the challenges.

Fast forward to today. In the last decade, I've been busy. Keep in mind: I began my first business with literally zero experience in online business – and I mean, *none*, other than a marketing and management degree that was purely theory-based. But it hasn't stopped me.

I have:

- Launched a sold-out swimwear collaboration with It Girl, Matilda Djerf. She was unbelievably sweet and humble when we worked together, and it was so successful she signed on to launch a second collection with me.
- Been noticed by New York Fashion Week scouts (I know right. I'll share more on that experience later but talk about a 'pinch me' moment).
- After scaling up my swimwear label to a global brand, I went on to sell the business to an international buyer five years later.

- Featured in *Forbes* magazine for my expertise in growing and scaling businesses – not once, or twice, but three times.
- Founded an influencer travel agency, taking top influencers on luxurious trips all around the world, promoting destinations and brands.
- Built a bricks and mortar events and photography venue, which was booked out every single weekend.
- Selected as a finalist in the Telstra Women in Business Awards in 2017 and a winner of the Telstra Business Awards and Westpac Businesses of Tomorrow Awards in 2018.

In the last few years, I've successfully built from scratch and grown my mentoring business, which provides a continually growing income, month after month after month, not to mention the pure fulfilment I get every single day.

**I get to be paid to be ME — all of me,
including my expertise and experience — doing
what I love and helping other women
hit their next-level business goals.**

I've studied and achieved almost a dozen life coaching and mindset certifications in multiple modalities, including Neuro Linguistic Programming and Human Design certifications. And now, I'm taking everything I've learnt running my businesses together with all my training and credentials, to help other people just like you to create amazing levels of success in their businesses.

If someone had told me ten years ago where I would be today and showed me a glimpse of the wild leaps I would undertake, the opportunities I created for myself, the incredible highlights, and the moments I backed myself against all odds. I would have been very surprised but also thought, *'Well, of course you did'*.

Let's Talk About You

If you picked up this book, then you've probably got big goals and dreams for yourself. And you've probably never been one to 'play small' either.

> **I'm going to assume that you're ready to make a change. That you want to experience wild success (more than you perhaps already have done), and sometimes that is the thing that scares you the most.**

Wherever you are on your business journey, some of my story likely resonates with you. We've all had those moments where we think, *Screw it, let's just burn it all to the ground*; or *What am I doing here?*

I hope that after reading this book those days will be behind you. *Way* back in your rear-view mirror. Because you'll be just as convinced as I am in your ability to succeed, and you'll have the same level of irrational, unequivocal self-belief that I do. Even if it feels like there are 108,000 reasons why not, or the challenges in your way seem insurmountable.

This book is for you – the big dreamer, the one who never takes no for an answer – so that you too can find a way to MAKE IT HAPPEN and experience unstoppable success. I'm going to show you how to go deep and do the inner work that's needed to shake off any of those subconscious limiting beliefs so you can get out of your way and take BOLD action.

Yes, you're going to have to step – actually, LEAP – outside of your comfort zone, and it probably won't feel great at first. It might feel uncomfortable, unfamiliar, or even downright painful to let go. But what I can promise you is that you already have the ability to create massive success within you. It's right there, waiting to be uncovered.

You can Create Your Reality

By now, you're probably starting to understand that I believe you have the power to create absolutely any reality you dream of. But first, you need to believe it's possible for you. So, I'm going to level with you. We don't need to spend time picking apart all the reasons 'why not'. In this book, I'm going to give you a massive kick up the butt and remind you, through the lessons and advice and practical tools and tips, that *anything is possible for you.*

The reality is that you already have everything you need to create success within you.

If you feel like right now your goals are a little out of reach or it's not possible for you or you're not capable, I want you to know that you can create the life of your wildest freaking dreams. Or maybe you *do* believe in yourself. Maybe you know what you want, and you really want to reach for the stars, but you want to set your goals even higher, dream even bigger, and get rid of any last sabotaging mindsets and beliefs that keep you stuck. Whatever your starting point, I'm going to share some of the hard-won lessons I've learnt and pay forward some of the incredible advice, tips and strategies I've picked up on my journey.

I'm very privileged in the position I'm in today. I accept and acknowledge the leg-up I had simply from being born in Australia, with access to basic healthcare and education and a loving family home.

I didn't grow up in a wealthy family and I've created my success. I didn't do anything crazy to make millions of dollars. And I didn't do anything to create this level of wealth that you can't do yourself. I've learnt how to work in a way that is more efficient, more effective, more potent, and more powerful. These results are what's possible when you have absolute, deep-down belief, and your brain doesn't even entertain the idea of not being successful. Because it just *knows* it's possible.

As well as a deep positive mindset and self-belief (which I'm going to help you with in the chapters ahead), you also need some simple business systems to help propel you forward with action. You can't sit at home and wait for money and opportunities to magically land in your lap, you need to take action to make it all happen.

You can Unlock a Whole New Level of Overflowing Success

You might know this saying: if nothing changes, then nothing changes.

I believe the only way to get a different result is to do things differently – and that's the whole purpose of this book. So, as you are reading through these pages, I want you to throw out the ideas you currently hold around what works and what doesn't – and just be open to the possibility of what *could be*. I am here to challenge your thinking, push you out of your comfort zone and help you make some wild things happen.

In just seven potent years, I've accomplished unstoppable success and I'm ready to share it all. Again, don't get me wrong: it wasn't all smooth sailing. The past seven years in business have by no means been a clear path, but I wouldn't change a single thing. I've met with a million 'noes', have had numerous people underestimate me, cried countless tears, and experienced the occasional moments of self-doubt and fear of being judged and seen. I've had many setbacks, but the key to my success is that I didn't let any of that stop me. Not for one second. I kept getting back up and trying something new.

I've always kept going. And now, I want to share with you how I have created success in both my business and personal life. So, whatever your goals are right now, I urge you to take it one step further – *dream a little LOT bigger*. If this excites you, GREAT. If it scares you, EVEN BETTER.

The only thing stopping you from having the success you desire is YOU.

I'm going to support you on this journey and help you work through the fears, limiting beliefs and blocks that are standing in your way. I'm going to help you to stop 'playing it safe'. I'm going to help you achieve your goals as you work towards huge levels of success – the kind of levels that you have only ever dreamt of or maybe haven't even allowed yourself to dream of yet. I chose this path because I always knew there was a way and if there wasn't a way, I made my own. This is your sign to pave your path and make those goals happen – because there is always a way.

Key Insights

- Unshakeable self-belief means you have so much trust in your ability to make it work, that you can take the leap, even when you don't know how it will work out.

- You're going to have to step – actually, DIVE – outside of your comfort zone, and it probably won't feel great at first. It might feel uncomfortable, unfamiliar, or even downright painful to let go.

- You already have the ability to create massive success within you. It's right there, waiting to be uncovered.

- You can't sit at home and wait for money and opportunities to magically land in your lap; you need to take action to make it all happen.

If you can achieve your goals sooner, why wait? Why do we focus on the roadblocks rather than focusing on the goals or opportunities that we have in front of us?

CHAPTER 2

Your New Superpowers

I remember sitting in the backseat of the family car, driving past a bank, and saying to my parents, 'I need to go to the bank.' 'What for, Jess?' I mean, why on earth would a 12-year-old need to go to the bank? I replied, 'To buy a house.'

I can't remember why I was so excited to get into the property market as a child, but I *do* remember having an unshakeable confidence and conviction that buying a house was what I wanted to do. So, I was going to do it.

Now, buying a house at the age of 12 doesn't make a lot of sense. But you never know what planting a seed might lead to.

What you believe becomes your reality, and realising your wildest dreams begins with a belief that anything is possible.

The lesson that I've learnt from my younger self is to lean into the illogical, the delusional, BIG ideas and with an unshakeable belief that I can make it happen against all odds. You've got to be a little delusional – or a lot – if you want to create wild success.

Embracing Delusional Thinking

I've always pursued my dreams with unshakeable belief and faith that when I leap, only good things can happen.

It's the reason why I have created so much success in all my businesses, even when it makes absolutely NO LOGICAL SENSE. For example, one week before I was about to deliver my first TEDx talk, I had a professional speaking expert tell me point-blank that I was not ready and that I had a long way to go before I would be ready for the TEDx stage. Much to their surprise, I responded with 'I am doing it next week' and I walked onto that stage nailing the delivery. If I had listened to logic or the 'experts' who told me I wasn't ready, I wouldn't be a TEDx speaker today. Now, some might say this is a delusional way of thinking. To those people, I say: it sure is.

Being delusional is having an unshakable belief when almost everyone else believes it to be false.

I don't know about you, but I sure as hell want to be so grounded and convicted in my abilities, so that even when everyone says it can't be done, I say, 'Just watch me'. When I look around me, I can see it's clear that the biggest success stories, the most impactful entrepreneurs, and the change-makers who create new ways of doing things all have this 'delusional' quality in common.

This level of delusional thinking is what I call, playing in Fantasy Land. It's a place where anything and everything is possible; where there are no rules and where you can achieve all your wildest dreams. When you embrace this way of thinking and combine it with taking bold action, you become unstoppable in your pursuit of success.

Playing in Fantasy Land is ...

- Having the BOLD CONFIDENCE to go after what you want.

- Taking a huge LEAP OF FAITH, even when people think you're crazy.

- Having the deepest SELF-TRUST so that when people say 'no', you say 'just watch me'.

- Going balls to the wall TOWARDS YOUR GOALS, because you're not afraid of skinning your knees along the way.

- Facing challenges HEAD-ON, knowing that no matter what, you can find a way forward.

- Having the courage to DREAM BIG, because you already know what you're capable of.

- Enjoying the SUCCESS you've created for yourself – knowing you earned it.

Think about a time in the past when you dared to leap into your goals with bold confidence. This is the energy you'll want to bring as you work through this book.

When I first met Ez, she was a musician with a vision. She was successful and well known in the wedding music industry and she knew she was capable of so much more. This is her story:

Ez was frustrated with the wedding industry's approach to incorporating live music into these events. Talented musicians were being paid poorly and struggling to find paid gigs. Ez wanted to change the way the whole system worked. She wasn't just here to sing and play music – she was ready to change and disrupt an entire industry.

Some people might see this as a monumental task, with a whole lot of delusion. Taking on an entire industry would be no small feat, but Ez was ready to play in Fantasy Land where anything and everything is possible.

Ez's goal was to start an instant-booking musician agency. It had never been done before and the current industry was stuck in their old ways of manual bookings, underpaying their talent, and making it hard for clients to find and book amazing musicians. She had a delusional vision and self-belief, but she was unclear about how to make it a reality.

Initially, we worked on the strategy, implementation, and marketing plans to make it a huge success. Ez has owned her vision and created an in-demand, exclusive agency that has raised the standard in the industry. She has a line-up of talented musicians who have secured hundreds of additional gigs. Three years in a row, Ez and her agency won the nationwide Australian Wedding Awards.

But she didn't stop there. Ez often sends me voice memos of her newest grand ideas. In less than two years she's built her wildly successful agency, continued to grow her musical success, and started a new business, Gig School, teaching other musicians to finally ditch the 'broke musician' narrative, get paid well and secure major gigs.

She is now on her most delusional yet magical Fantasy Land mission yet: she is taking her business to the next level by becoming certified so that she can issue industry-recognised certifications. Ez knows the absolute value and results her programs create and she's ready to compete directly with the top universities in the country.

Ez had approached me for business growth and had created a whole new level of success, impact and dreaming bigger than she had ever imagined.

As with all my clients I had challenged Ez to play bigger and create the life of her dreams, to step out of her comfort zone in the most expansive way and build her legacy. Stepping into Fantasy Land for Ez, started with the question: 'How can I …?'. When you lead with this question, it opens you up to all the opportunities in front of you. This goes way beyond just growing a business, making some money, or improving mindset; all of that happens too, but it's so much more than that.

The One Thing Standing Between You and Success

I want you to do a little exercise with me. It'll only take two minutes, I promise. Close your eyes and think back for a moment to when you were young. I'm talking *really* little – around the time you started school for the first time.

Maybe you were five years old, and you begged your parents for the Barbie Dream House that was advertised on the TV in between the Saturday morning cartoons. Or you might have asked if you could have your birthday party at McDonald's to celebrate with all your friends. Or you desperately wanted a special doll, truck or toy. You didn't care (or even know) about the price tag. You never doubted that you *deserved* the things you wanted, right? All that was standing between you and the things your heart truly desired were your parents and their willingness to say yes. No thoughts like *'But I'm not worthy of that'* or *'I don't deserve that'* crossed your mind. Because 'little you' had total and complete faith and self-belief to ask for anything you wanted.

Fast forward, however, many years to the 'you' you are today, and things are a little different. There are all sorts of beliefs and stories we tell ourselves (unconsciously or consciously) about what we think we can and can't do or accomplish with this one life we have. So, here's my question for you. If 'little you' believed you could do anything, be anything and have anything ... what changed? The answer is simple ... You did. It's not your bank balance, or your relationship status, or how well-connected your family is. It's YOU.

You see, we're all born without any conditioning. When we're young, we believe that anything is possible. We believe in the Tooth Fairy, the Easter Bunny and Santa Claus. We believe we can wish upon a star and the wish will come true We believe we could fly if we could just concentrate hard enough. Somewhere along the way, you decided that you don't quite deserve what others have. That pure light core of belief was dampened and then lost. But the reality is, right now, whatever your age and life stage, the same principles of belief are at play. You were born with everything you need to succeed. And now, it's your time and obligation to step into it and claim that next level.

When you trust yourself fully, that's when you really start to see magic happen.

What you believe becomes your reality, and realising your wildest dreams begins with a belief that anything is possible. Five-year-old you thought this was true – why don't you? Some of us have been able to hold on to these childlike beliefs that we can create, achieve, and accomplish anything we set our minds to – maybe this is you. This is my mindset; I am living proof of the fact that we can create illogical levels of success in our lives.

Don't Wait Until You're 'Ready'

Does it make any sense whatsoever that I was invited to show my swimwear label at New York Fashion Week after just one week of launching my business? Yes, just one week.

It all started with an intention and deep belief in what I was creating. I set my intention to create a global fashion brand from day one – a brand that would rival the top players. There wasn't one ounce of me that didn't see that becoming my reality, even though I had no evidence for it to be true. With that deep belief and conviction, I began taking action towards those goals in a big way: marketing, photoshoots, all of it in a way that positioned me as a category leader.

I launched the brand in February 2016 after five busy months my swimwear was available, finally live and online, and just one week later, *it* happened. I was sitting at my desk at my marketing job, secretly tending to my business on the side as you do (well, I did. I certainly was not winning any employee of the year awards). I opened my phone to check my emails and saw a subject line: 'Invitation to showcase at New York Fashion Week'. When I first read it, I thought it was spam. Or a scam. Or someone was playing a prank. Why would I be approached by NYFW with an *out of this world* opportunity to showcase my brand on the world stage when I was a virtual unknown?

I jumped into research mode to see if this was a genuine offer. The email mentioned a bunch of brands that had been invited to show at NYFW the previous year, so I started contacting them to see if the story was legit. Turns out – it was! I could feel the excitement start to build as it began to dawn on me that this was a genuine opportunity. But let's keep in mind that at this point, I had never run a business in my life. I had a huge vision for this swimwear brand, but I was still learning all the logistics. I had no idea how to optimise our manufacturing processes, and I had just spent my life savings on creating this first ever collection, getting the business up and running and marketing the brand.

And suddenly, New York Fashion Week was calling. That said, there are so many logical, sensible, totally practical reasons why I could have (and many would say, should have) passed up that opportunity. I could've said, 'Thank you but no thank you'. And no one would have blamed me because my reasons for saying no would have been legitimate. Many, many valid reasons such as …

I don't have the time. I had just launched and was running the business while still working full-time in my marketing job, pulling 90-hour weeks on the regular – and now, I was being asked to create a whole new collection from concept and design to manufacturing and showing. Oh, yeah – and I only had six months to pull it off.

I don't have the money. I genuinely didn't. My life savings were gone, remember? And guess what? A global fashion show costs money for manufacturing plus travel plus branding plus marketing plus logistics.

I don't know how to. I'd never pulled together a fashion show in my life. And now I had to figure out how to create a dynamic fashion show that would knock the socks off the audience in New York.

I don't have a collection to show. Oh, yeah, that pesky little detail! I had just exhausted all my ideas in the launch of my very first collection. And have I mentioned that I hadn't even sold many swimsuits yet? And here was NYFW, knocking on my door, asking me to make a brand-new collection in less than six months. For those of you who aren't familiar with the fashion industry, let's just say, that's a really short timeframe.

I don't belong here, alongside brands that are way more established and 'credible'. I was invited to showcase and appear on that runway alongside prominent Australian brands I had long admired.

Okay, I think you get the picture by now – there were so many reasons why it would've been the easier choice to decline this opportunity. But I think you know enough about me by now to realise that nothing was going to stop me. This was a once-in-a-lifetime opportunity. So, I said yes. Signed a contract. Then I strapped myself in for a wild ride and figured out the rest along the way.

I'm all for leaping before you are ready, saying yes and simply finding a way to make it work. And it did. Like I always say: where there's a will, there's a way. I'm sharing all of this with you as a reminder that your goal doesn't have to make logical sense for it to be possible for you. So, you should take that leap – even if you think you're not ready. Even if you think you should wait. Even if it makes *total sense* for you to wait. None of it would have happened at all if I wasn't brave enough to take action before I was ready.

Too often, I see people wait until they're 'ready' to take that next step:

- Until they're a bit more confident.
- Until they have more experience under their belt.
- Until they've worked with X number of clients.

- Until they've achieved a certain number of sales or have a specific amount of money in the bank.
- Until they have their full pitch ready.
- Until, until, until …

The lesson here? 'Until' might never happen. So, take action before you're ready because you'll figure it out as you go. Remember you ARE already an entrepreneur, a Fantasy Land chaser, you have the experience, this is about moving away from the negative into your unstoppable, successful, self. If you can achieve your goals sooner, why wait? Why do we focus on the roadblocks rather than focusing on the goals or opportunities that we have in front of us?

Believe the Impossible

I believe that truly anything is possible if *you* believe it is. Here are some things you could do in your life that you might not have believed were possible; you could:

- Work fewer hours or work any hours you choose.
- Earn more money – the limit is uncapped.
- Have more fun (whatever your definition of fun is).
- Be featured in the media and quoted as an expert in your field.
- Go on incredible adventures you've been dreaming about for years.
- Partner with brands and events that make your heart sing.
- Embrace and engage support to make your life easier and more seamless.
- Spend more time (and quality time) with your loved ones.

- Level up your lifestyle in a way that aligns with your values.
- Embrace flow and ease in your business and your life.
- Have a deeper impact on the communities you serve.

And guess what? You can have all the above and more. I don't believe we have to sacrifice or choose just one.

Now it's your turn:

When I'm working with my clients on this exercise I like to start with a reflection or journalling prompt. In your journal write down all your impossible goals, the big ones you want to chase, and how you could achieve the outcomes.

The most common impossible goal I hear is that earning more means you would have to sacrifice your time with your family. What if instead, you could have more of both?

Ask for What You Want

Once you step into your delusional self-belief and set your sights on your big goals, it's time to make them happen!

Every single opportunity I've had, every win I've enjoyed and every piece of success I have achieved I went out and created for myself. It's a strategy that has paid off time and time again. I mean, we've all heard the phrase 'if you don't ask, you won't get'. But is it just another cute quote that's sitting on your vision board? Or is it something you boldly live by? I'm telling you right now – anything you can dream of is possible. You can't wait for opportunities to land in your lap – you need to go out and *get it*. Take a grip of your delusional, Fantasy Land mindset and LEAP.

Back in 2018, I set myself a huge goal. I had a dream to work with a major retailer. I'm talking huge: think, they're in almost every shopping mall in Australia. I was so delusional that NOT working with them didn't even cross my mind. The way my brain works is like this: once I know what I want, I figure out a way to make it happen.

First, I needed a contact. I knew absolutely no one in the industry who could offer an introduction, but remember, where there's a will there's always a way. I hit up every single person I could find on LinkedIn who worked for this retail group. A few days later, I followed up with all of them. And a week later, after hearing nothing back– I followed up again.

I was persistent because I had a brilliant idea for a collaboration that I just knew would be a perfect fit for their brand. So, I kept asking. I finally received a response, from the head of the product department, the exact person I needed to connect with, and she agreed to a meeting. The company was in Melbourne, and, as fate would have it, I was at the airport preparing to fly there when I received confirmation of our meeting. I couldn't pass up the opportunity to meet in person, so I pushed for a meeting immediately, and she agreed to give me 15 minutes.

Before the meeting, a friend gave me a brilliant piece of advice: 'Don't go into this meeting and talk solely about you,' my friend said. 'Instead, ask about them and see what problems you can help them solve.' This one little piece of 'communication magic' has helped me through so many negotiations, so many sales, and so many collaborations. I threw that 'me pitch' out the window and went in with a whole new approach. I opened our conversation by asking about their pain points and our discussion provided insights on how I could help solve their concerns and provide value to their business with my idea.

Asking people what you can do for them is a powerful way to build trust and rapport during important conversations.

We ended up speaking for 40 minutes (sometimes all you need is a foot in the door and a new approach). My friend was right. When you truly understand the needs and desires of your dream clients, or in my case dream brand partners, it allows you to craft your messaging and offer to suit their needs all the while building trust and real connections, rather than coming in hot with a pitch based on assumptions. Over the next few weeks, we had multiple meetings, and we were so close to launching a partnership.

Together we crafted the products and discussed the logistics, profit margins, and all the elements that were needed to launch. Then, a very last-minute change in strategy from the leadership team saw them hit the big, fat pause button on collaborations with outside brands. Sadly, the deal was over. But my time hadn't been wasted – not in the slightest. I still consider that experience to be a massive win. It was one of the biggest growth opportunities of my life.

I had launched myself out of my comfort zone. I made some fantastic new connections. I learnt some amazing negotiation skills that continue to serve me to this day, and I confirmed for myself that being tenacious is a key strategy for getting ahead.

I'm proud of myself for taking the leap and making contact in the first place – for daring to ask, for making the meetings happen and for believing it was all possible.

Emilee, one of my clients, did exactly this. She stepped into her delusional, Fantasy Land mindset way before she felt ready – with epic results:

> Emilee had launched a product-based business and was struggling with self-belief, to the point where she was still working her full-time job while getting her business off the ground. Straight up, I coached her on making a big decision: are you going all-in on the business? Or are you keeping it as a side hustle? She was playing small and waiting 'until' something happened to make her feel comfortable turning this from a passion into a purpose.
>
> After our session, Emilee decided she wanted to go all-in, she had enough of playing small. That led me to my next question: what are your big, crazy, Fantasy Land goals for not just making your business a huge success but making it the business of your wildest dreams? What would that look like? What would you achieve? Who would your clients be? How much money would you make each month?
>
> I love to test people's thought processes and with Emilee, I could see she was getting in her way and blocking what was truly possible. Once we lifted those blinkers, she was able to clearly see the big vision for her business and create massive goals around what she truly wanted.
>
> 'I want a huge partnership,' she told me during our next coaching session. 'I want to partner with a major brand and achieve massive awareness for my business.' I helped

her step into that 'big-brand energy' and crafted a major strategy and action plan to make it all happen. This is the type of delusional thinking that can take you places. I prompted her further. 'Who would your dream partner be? And what would the partnership look like?'

Emilee and I began brainstorming and together we created a 'big picture' list of brands that could be ideal partners. Now, that list was important but what was even more important was developing Emilee's self-belief. She stepped into the core concept that asking for what you want is absolutely okay and set her sights firmly on achieving her big goals. And, while I held her accountable, it was up to Emilee to bite the bullet and reach out and make that brand-enhancing partnership happen. And then, what do you know? One of them replied.

As a result, Emilee and her newfound self-belief and big-picture confidence had sponsored a high-profile nationwide event with an audience of thousands in each market, for a total investment of ... wait for it ... zero dollars.

Her logo was featured alongside airline Jetstar and other major lifestyle and finance brands. Her involvement created extensive awareness for her brand, and she captured a tonne of high-quality content to share on her social media for months to come.

When you're inspired to move out of your comfort zone and lead with a penetrating vision, you will move forward from dabbling in a business to playing in the big league. Emilee has now taken a massive leap forward in her business, simply because she allowed herself to play in Fantasy Land – and then she took bold action towards making it happen.

What are you waiting for?

Ask yourself:

> Are you playing in Fantasy Land? If not, why not?
> What's holding you back?
> What situations are you avoiding?
> What meetings haven't you asked for?
> What projects haven't you started?
> What goals are you putting off?

In your journal, write down a list of at least five things you've held off doing:

- Next to each of these five items, write down the reason WHY you haven't taken action. Now cross all those reasons out (I'm serious) because they're often just excuses keeping you safe.

- Now, set yourself a task for each goal and take that leap. You're the only one who is going to make it happen!

- If you are unsure of the next steps finding a mentor or someone successful, that you align with, could provide a shortcut to making it happen.

And keep reading – we have some great tools and tips coming your way.

_____

Do You Need a Mentor?

A business mentor is someone with experience and skills who can support you, act as a sounding board, and help you overcome challenges on your business journey. They can give you new ideas, encourage you when you're down and share their expertise.

A mentor can provide a shortcut to success, pushing you when you're playing small – they can help you fast-track your growth and build a bridge to your beliefs, in a way that helps you feel safe and supported. Most importantly they should align with your values and goals:

- Have they achieved the version of success you desire?

- Is there expertise in an area that you find challenging?

- Do your values align with theirs so they can guide you to what is right for you?

- Do they practise what they preach and lead by example?

- What is the level of support you are seeking? Some mentors will be more accessible than others.

- Do they challenge you to get out of your comfort zone?

A mentor could be one or many people. You may belong to a business growth group which is great but having that one-on-one, focused energy all about you can be game-changing.

It's All in Your Mindset

One huge reason why some people have more success than others is their mindset.

Now, you might be thinking: okay, cool, but what is mindset? And why can't we skip ahead, and you just give me the strategy for success? Here's the hot tip – working on your mindset IS the strategy for success. And no, I'm not talking about positive affirmations in the mirror or pure love and light. I am talking about truly understanding how your brain and subconscious work, so you can unlock insane next levels of success and stop blocking yourself (we'll get to that in Chapter 4).

While I believe you *can* create massive levels of success without ever having completed the inner work, we all have a different level of self-belief and different stories we tell ourselves on the daily. These stories shape our habits and behaviours, which in turn shape our reality. What I have discovered is that when you remove all the rules of what you 'think' is possible, the world truly opens up for you in all of its infinite possibilities. And in the pages ahead, we're going to deep dive into mindset and the ways you can wildly transform your results, your success, and your entire life. But first, a mini-neuroscience lesson so we're all starting on the same page.

We each have a conscious and subconscious mind. Dr Bruce Lipton, a professor at Stanford University Medical Center and expert on the power of your subconscious mind, says it is a million times more powerful than the conscious mind, we operate 95 to 99% of our lives from subconscious programs.

Translation: you're not consciously aware of the habits you're forming, the behaviours you're adopting or the decisions you're making, because it's all happening subconsciously.

Think about this: how would you even consciously think about keeping your heart beating, if it wasn't happening automatically? How would we get anything done if we had to focus on telling our eyelids to blink every few seconds? Taking just one step activates 200 muscles in your body – if we were operating from our conscious mind all the time, even walking to the mailbox would be a massive effort.

Operating from our subconscious can be a good thing. As Tim Ash explains in his book *Unleash Your Primal Brain*, it all goes back to caveman days when our ancestors' brains were moulded by 'ruthless survival pressures from the earliest days of life on the planet'. Back then, subconscious thinking helped to preserve and protect us – and those ways of thinking are still inside of us. Here's a quick example. Countless studies show that most people are afraid of public speaking, research from the University of Florida suggests around 75% feel like this. Let's say you're in this camp.

You are offered an opportunity to present in front of a group at an upcoming event, it is going to be a massive opportunity to showcase your business and grow your brand. But the idea of getting up to speak in front of people makes you sweat just thinking about it, so you're terrified about saying yes. Your subconscious brain recognises your fear and instantly goes into 'protective mode'. It doesn't know the difference between a *real* threat, and the ones we face in our journey toward success.

Your subconscious is purely focused on keeping you safe and is operating in the background without any conscious awareness of the self-sabotage playing out behind the scenes. It tells you that you can't possibly say yes to this opportunity, for about a thousand reasons, which your brain is helpfully coming up with for you.

It just won't work because:

- The event is too soon.
- You don't have enough time to prepare.
- The audience isn't quite the right fit.
- You already have plans that day.
- The time of the speaking gig is inconvenient.
- Your website isn't ready yet.

You could come up with *all* the reasons why it makes sense to say 'thanks but no thanks' to this opportunity. And those excuses might feel valid, comfortable, and safe. But they'll keep you stuck exactly where you are right now and most of the time, you won't even realise. It's the reason why, sometimes, no matter how much you want to achieve a goal, you keep hitting roadblocks, plateau, self-sabotage, and keep coming up against the exact same issues. You need to tackle and shift those unconscious beliefs. And in the next few chapters, I'm going to show you exactly how to do it.

Key Insights

- You were born with everything you need to succeed. When you trust yourself fully, that's when you really start to see magic happen.

- By definition, being delusional is having an unshakable belief in something, when almost everyone else views this belief to be false.

- The biggest success stories, the most impactful entrepreneurs and the change-makers who created new ways of doing things all had this 'delusional' quality in common.

- Literally anything you can dream of is possible for you – but if you don't ask, you won't get it.

- Take action before you're ready. You'll figure it out as you go.

- Your subconscious mind is running the show over 90% of the time. Is your subconscious working in your best interests?

**I have discovered that when you remove
all the rules of what you 'think' is possible,
the world truly opens up for you in all
of its infinite possibilities.**

**Your version of success doesn't have to
make logical sense to be possible for you.
The bigger, bolder and more outrageous
your dreams, the better!**

CHAPTER 3

Getting Set Up for Success

I'm going to be straight with you: my version of success is *not* having a million dollars in the bank at all costs.

Don't get me wrong – I like banking those zeros. And having a six-figure month in my business is truly satisfying. But the *real* flex is not having to hustle to make it happen. A six-figure month that involves me working 100 hours a week, sacrificing all my personal time, neglecting my health and sleep, and managing a big team of staff ... no thanks! There are successful business owners who work so hard to earn major levels of wealth, only to box themselves into a high stress, exhausting corporate role they wanted to get out of. Nope, that's not my vibe. And it's definitely not my idea of success.

Personally, my idea of success is working *less* for *more*. It's having huge financial breakthroughs and making more money than I ever imagined, without burning myself out along the way. It took me a long time to realise this. For so long, I used to sit in a freezing cold, air-conditioned office and wish I was outside at the beach. So, I started my own business to give me that flexibility. Yet in the early stages, I ended up working more than ever, and subsequently even further from that reality.

I ran my swimwear brand for five years and only went to the beach a couple of times a year – mostly for brand photoshoots. I was running five businesses at once and running myself into the ground at the same time. I became 'too busy' and made many sacrifices in my personal life because, at the time, I subscribed to hustle culture at all costs. I remember the moment I realised something had to change.

My businesses were all booked out, sold out and thriving ... but I certainly wasn't. I was almost at my breaking point (again). I would wake up and immediately pick up my phone and solve whatever issue happened overnight in one of my companies. I was in a frantic frenzy all day, likely forgetting to eat breakfast until 3 pm – sometimes I didn't even get out of my PJs because I was 'too busy'. Not surprisingly I hit the breaking point again. I arrived at my office and straight into a major conflict in one of my businesses. I went into a full-blown anxiety attack, my entire body felt like it was going to combust. If you've ever had an anxiety attack before, you know what I mean when I say I could no longer function.

At that moment, I knew something needed to change. I asked myself one simple question: what does TRUE success look like to me if there were no expectations or rules? My answer was very clear. I needed to come first if I was ever going to create sustainable lasting success. I hope you *never* reach this point. Having this experience is why I am so passionate about empowering you to chase YOUR version of success. There I was with what should have been everything I'd been working towards. I had wildly successful companies: I had the clients, the money, and the recognition to go with it. But that simply wasn't 'success' to me.

Is your current business serving you?

On the journey to success, it is important to check in with yourself regularly to ensure you are still aligned with the path you want to be on. Often, at the start of our entrepreneurial journey we are eager to dive into taking action. However, over time, we may veer off course and find ourselves in a different place.

Take a moment to reflect and audit your day-to-day life, the way you operate your business, how many hours you are working and how it makes you feel. Using your journal, make a list of what is no longer serving you and set an intention for how it needs to change.

On my journey towards 'slowing down', focusing on my health and filling my days with doing things I love, I've become 100% laser-focused on what success *really* looks like to me. Hint: it's not a corner suite in a fancy office, overseeing a big team and working long hours. I exited those businesses – even though they were very lucrative – and chose *my* version of success. Now that I work from home, if I want to have a bath at 3 pm (like I often do), I can. If I want to structure my meetings so the afternoon is free to go to the beach, I will. If I feel like planning a couple of days off to disappear for a long weekend with my partner, I do.

And it all happens with ease and simplicity. There are no stressful late nights, trying to cram in all my work so I can 'buy myself' a Friday and Monday away from my desk. Having that freedom and flexibility to work with my energy and do what I feel I want to do is so key for me – it is the absolute definition of success. I have structured my coaching business in a way that allows me to make a huge impact, while also prioritising ease and flow and allowing time for myself, too. Before you think it's only me and my business model that makes this possible, I want to share that I've helped many of my clients achieve the same in e-commerce and services like photographers, marketing agencies and more.

Now, it's not about having to play smaller or sacrifice those big goals you have your sights set on, it's learning how to create a business model that allows you to have it all and be truly in alignment with your definition of success. I've worked out that I value keeping my business lean and exclusive. I have an intimate group of clients because I love and prefer close relationships and high-end personalised experiences. I assist my clients to develop this type of structure.

I have, at times, sacrificed potential income to stay in integrity and alignment with my vision and the way I want to lead my business, yet found that returns to me tenfold in the long term. I also run my business super lean, which means I have minimal expenses. So many business owners make lots of money, but not profit because they follow the usual business advice and scale their resources or make lots of hires to grow.

This is perfectly okay if it aligns with your business plan and helps set you up to smash your goals – just make sure you're not being misguided by what you 'think' success is. I've learnt that I can structure my business so that my work hours are the same, no matter how many zeros land in my bank account each month. If anything, I'm working fewer hours than I was before, while my income continues to increase. At one point, I went from 15 VIP one on one clients to five, and my income remained the same. Not only was I able to provide my clients a greater experience but I also had more time for me. I truly have invested in building a Business for Life where I am creating massive levels of success, impact and freedom while having minimal stress and burnout.

A girl's got big dreams and goals, and I'm here to do it sustainably for the long term.

For example, at the end of 2022, I had already secured substantial contracts/revenue for 2023 and the year hadn't even begun yet. The best part? Those contracts would only require 40 working hours to fulfil – not per week, for the entire year – providing me with time, space, freedom, and ease in my calendar. Now of course that was my baseline. I chose to undertake other projects over and above those 40 hours such as my weekly podcasts, creating content, working on fun projects, and creating new offers to leave my legacy. Imagine for a minute the possibilities that can open up if you let go of the idea that goals have to always make logical sense.

As I reflect on what I have built, it doesn't seem that long ago that I was working 40 hours per week and barely making one-third of that income. Big things can change fast for you too, when you allow yourself to define your version of success without limits.

What Does Your Version of Success Look Like?

It's not uncommon to set goals for 'things' rather than outcomes. For example, a client once told me: 'I want to gain 10,000 followers'. That's the *thing* she wanted to achieve. But why? What do the followers mean on their own? What is the outcome? What is the impact? Does she want a higher number on her follower count? That doesn't serve a purpose beyond boosting your ego for a moment with a hit of validation. Or is the actual goal to build a community that trusts her and purchases from her, so she can increase income and do what she loves every day?

When we chase 'things' rather than outcomes, it overcomplicates our business. We end up wasting time and energy while being no closer to our goals. It's like arriving at the airport for your vacation, boarding the plane and arriving at your destination, only to find out that you are on the wrong plane and the destination you dreamt of was in a different country altogether. You did the 'thing'– you boarded a plane and flew somewhere – but the end goal is nowhere to be seen. Now you've spent more money and time diverting from your path altogether.

We can also end up chasing the wrong 'things'. Business owners, even aspiring visionary CEOs and entrepreneurs, can grapple with a lack of clarity around the direction they should take. Instead of aligning with their authentic vision, some might try to replicate another person's definition of success, business model or strategy, rather than aligning it with their truth. This happens when we don't have trust in ourselves and feel more confident turning to external sources for guidance. We can end up taking a little too much inspiration or even just feel society's subconscious pressures to show success in a certain way.

Exhibit A: an expensive, designer car.

Someone you know is driving around town in a brand-new Porsche, splashing photos all over social media and generally having the time of their lives in their fancy new European sports car. Now for some, owning a luxury car is the absolute pinnacle of success and achievement. It's a sign that they've 'made it', a key to an exclusive club and an uplevelling in lifestyle that they relish.

For others, cars are simply not a high value. They'd rather not invest in a depreciating asset and they're happy enough with their second-hand wheels. Aka me, I drive my little old VW Polo (on the rare occasion I ever drive anywhere) and I have no plans to upgrade it any time soon. However, on the flip side, I will happily drop $50,000 on a luxury holiday because experiences and creating memories mean more to me than a fancy car.

Neither of these points of view is right or wrong. But they show you why it's important to get clear on *your* values. Once you know exactly what your idea of success is, you can set clear goals and then go after them.

Without clarity, it's way too easy to get caught up chasing metrics of success that don't matter to you.

In speaking to my coaching clients over the years and other women in business, I've discovered that their goals are often not 100% aligned to what they want. It's bound by what they think they *should* want, or some preconceived idea of what they *think* success looks like. As a result, they end up spending time, money, and energy in the wrong places. Correcting this imbalance is how I help my clients to collapse time around what is truly possible.

Marie is an incredible food photographer, but she was burnt out from working long hours chasing society's idea of success (being booked out) and couldn't see how to increase her income without overcommitting herself even more. This is her story:

Marie needed to completely transform her business model to allow for more income and more freedom. Her current offers, pricing and time capacity meant that she was capped with nowhere to grow. With a calendar that had limited availability for additional work we increased her pricing and created long-term retainer options for her clients. Marie was able to forecast her projects, earn more for the same time input and gain control over her schedule.

This is where the fear and self-sabotage crept in. Marie's biggest fear was that by increasing her prices, she would lose long-standing clients or income because of price objections. Every time I work with my clients on major growth and change it pushes them out of their comfort zone, but it's how they navigate that fear that matters. If you truly want to grow and reach a new level of success it will require you to be uncomfortable.

We worked together on overcoming those fears, digging deeper into Marie's self-sabotage, and building her self-confidence in her high quality of service. At the same time, we re-mastered her messaging and marketing so that it was speaking to high-end buyers. Marie then felt the fear and acted anyway. She sent her new prices to past and new clients, and guess what happened ... they signed up and paid and not one of them questioned or pushed back on the price.

Within just three months, she increased her income four times over and halved her working hours, with every Friday scheduled off work.

Read that again: over four times her income, half the work hours and she had every Friday to do whatever she wanted. And she achieved all of that in less than three months when previously she felt completely stuck and couldn't see a way forward. Marie had well and truly taken the wheel and with a little push, and a whole lot of unstoppable success, she was moving towards her goals and her version of success. Now that's what I call playing in Fantasy Land.

This is your proof that things can move very fast (without the hustle and burnout) when you're paying attention to the right things. But first, you need to dig deep and unearth your version of success, so you can then take big bold action toward it and forget the rest.

Before we move on, I want to give you a friendly reminder that your version of success doesn't have to make logical sense to be possible for you. The bigger, bolder, and more outrageous your dreams, the better. There will be mindset blocks that crop up when you begin to play in Fantasy Land and pursue those illogical goals. To move past these roadblocks, you need to understand why self-sabotage tends to play out for you in the specific ways that it does. This is personal to you and your values, beliefs, and true purpose. So, what can you do about it? I'm about to tell you.

Say No to Self-sabotage

I believe that self-sabotage does NOT exist – it's total bullshit. Unpopular opinion, I know, but I'm going to tell you why.

The whole purpose of your subconscious mind is to protect and help you. So why on earth would it go out of its way to sabotage you? It makes no sense whatsoever! What's really going on is a conflict of *values* and *goals*. Here's an example. Think about a time when you have felt like you were self-sabotaging. You know exactly what your goal is, but for some reason you're behaving in a different way that doesn't match the action you need to take to reach the goal … so it gets further and further out of reach.

For instance, you have a proposal you know you need to work on. It has the potential to land you a BIG client. A huge payday.

You're excited and every day you plan to work on it. But other urgent tasks get in the way and before you know it, another day ends and you haven't worked on this pitch, sent it off or made any progress whatsoever.

You go to bed feeling annoyed with yourself. Why is this happening? After all, your goal is to earn more money. This proposal could make you more money. So why do you keep procrastinating on it? What could be more important, more urgent, than landing a big client and making money? Well, there's one thing that could be more important: keeping you safe. And that's exactly what your subconscious mind is trying to do.

Your subconscious is going to show up like a loving, overbearing mum taking care of you. She's not here to sabotage you and make your life harder, but she runs on the stories you tell her.

If the story you're telling her is that the school friends you hang out with are putting you down and making you feel bad, then you better believe your protective subconscious is going to kick in and march down to that school, talk to the principal and demand action. The same way that if you tell her this Big Proposal you need to work on has the potential to land you a BIG client, which will create more work for you, put loads more pressure on your time, add to your stress levels and generally make life harder – she's going to step in and deal with it.

Remember: your brain wants to protect you. It wants to eliminate any threat. If Big New Client = Big Threat to your working hours and stress levels, then your subconscious will see this and show up as self-sabotage. Your SUBCONSCIOUS mind is trying to protect you from the threat (aka this Big Proposal).

But your CONSCIOUS mind sees it as procrastination or lack of motivation and keeps trying to push harder. You see the problem, right?

At this point, if there are elements of your business that do not support your values or the lifestyle you truly want, then no amount of pushing and motivation is going to get you there. Until you stop seeing 'procrastination' and 'lack of motivation' as the issue and start working toward the alignment of values and goals, it's going to be a constant uphill battle.

This goes back to our caveman days. Our brains are wired to protect us from danger and threats; we have inbuilt reactions to protect ourselves. Back in the day, those reactions were designed to save our lives. But our caveman's brain wasn't built to address the modern threats that you and I face every day or the modern lifestyles we lead. These days, many of the threats we face are emotional, psychological, and social. And that big old brain of yours? It can't tell the difference between these and the huge, scary physical threats our ancestors faced.

A threat is a threat. Whatever 'threat' comes your way, your caveman brain says, 'Nope, not a chance – we're not dealing with that. I'm going to help you get rid of this threat so you can be safe secure and happy. *You're welcome!*'

Creating Your Version of Success

So how do you stop this from happening and achieve your Fantasy Land levels of success?

Step 1: Get clear on your values

Values are your beliefs about what is important or desirable, they drive all your decisions and actions. The main reason that people fail to achieve their goals is that they don't understand their values and are unable to create goals with them in mind. It is integral to your unstoppable success that your values are fine-tuned. The more our achievements align with our values the more successful we feel.

Everyone's core values are unique and are more than likely wildly different to your partner, best friends, business mentor or loved one.

—— $\bigcirc$ ——

High visibility values

Start by daydreaming about your best and most successful life, and notice which words resonate when you're building this mental picture. What do you truly care about most in life?

You can also look to your past for clues; where did you feel most happy and fulfilled? Notice the words you associate with those moments and journal on this.

A few thought starters for you: achievement, freedom, travel, adventure, family, flow, charity, creativity, wealth, health ... the list is endless.

Now you have your values list, it's time to infuse them into your daily life until they become intrinsically you.

———————

Step 2: Live in alignment

Once you've decided on your values and exactly what your personal success looks like, start moving in that direction and inviting in opportunities to live in alignment with it. When setting your goals, take a balanced approach and make space for *all* your top values. This is how we create long-term, sustainable success.

For me, this initially meant scheduling more relaxation and more time for the beach and then fitting my business around that. It created safety for my subconscious to know that my health and well-being were sorted, even when I was working on my big business goals. I'm now at a point where my business flows seamlessly with ease around my lifestyle, as I'm living completely in alignment with *my* version of success.

Consider this example: If family is one of your top priority values and yet your current reality involves multitasking on your phone and chasing business goals during 'family time' you need to prioritise being fully present in those moments. Adjust how you allocate time to work on your business, optimise your processes, or even re-evaluate your business systems to ensure you can wholeheartedly engage in meaningful family moments.

Recognise that your values will be different to others, so it's essential to implement them in a way that truly serves you and aligns with your individual needs and aspirations.

It's time to make your values a priority

In your journal, write three intentions per value – do you want to be more present, do you want to do an activity more often, is it going to become a daily habit?

For example, one of my top values is adventure and when I am not travelling and fulfilling my adventure value in that way, I set an intention to take myself on spontaneous solo dates to local spots I have never been to before such as a new café, beach or just jump in the car and see where I end up. This always makes me feel more grounded and fulfilled.

Once you have set your intentions, schedule time for
each of your values into your calendar. By doing this,
you are making a commitment and reserving space
for the things that matter most to you. An intention
without a plan doesn't usually happen so this way you
are more likely to begin taking the steps toward your
dream life.

Now, we have the foundations to build your business
around your life, not the other way around.

Step 3. Dream up those Fantasy Land goals

This is where the fun really begins.

So far, we have spoken about the theory and you're now clear
on how (and why) your subconscious impacts your daily life, your
decisions and your ability to smash those big goals you set for
yourself. Now, it's time to put what you've learned into practice.

Reminder: there is no such thing as 'realistic'.

One of my biggest superpowers is working with powerhouse
business owners to reveal exactly what it is they really, truly
desire – and then crafting a direct path to attain that unstoppable
success. These paths can be different, of course, but they ALL
begin with the deep mindset work of developing unshakeable
self-belief.

The important part is that you need to step past the blockers
and 'unearth' your way of doing business and creating insane
success. Isabela is a perfect example of committing to this
experience and seeing the big dream outcomes, this is her story:

When Isabela was setting her goals for the new year,
she originally wanted to set a $500,000 income goal.

During our session, she asked me: 'Should I just choose something more realistic and set a goal of $200,000?'

While many other coaches and mentors will say, 'Set realistic goals, so you won't be disappointed or freak yourself out', you already know I'm not here to play small. 'If you never allow yourself to aim ridiculously high, then you are subconsciously capping your success and results,' I told her.

'If you set a $200,000 goal, guess what happens when you hit it? Your brain shuts off and you no longer absorb information that opens you up to opportunities of making your bigger $500,000 goal a reality, and your behaviours and actions play smaller at a $200,000 level.

'You are a big dreamer – you are a powerhouse and you're capable of insane levels of success. And whose definition of realistic are you using? To Kim Kardashian or Richard Branson, earning $200,000 in a day is perfectly realistic!' By the end of our pep talk, she'd locked in that $500,000 target. And guess what? She knocked it out of the park.

Whenever you are tempted to set smaller goals, it is only because your subconscious is keeping you safe – safe from the feeling that if you go for it and aim too high, and you don't achieve it, that will be embarrassing. I think it's more embarrassing to play small when you know you are capable of so much more. And remember when you set illogical, Fantasy Land goals, you are 100% more likely to hit something larger than if you settled for realistic.

Being confident in doing business *your way* is truly the key to unlocking huge levels of success. But before you know which way to go, you need to get to know yourself and what is going to work best for you. An integral part of creating unstoppable success is deep self-discovery, mindset, inner work, and understanding your strengths and values. This becomes your compass leading the way to success. The other part involves some level of trial and error. But believe me, without the compass, it's going to be a very choppy ride.

Your turn to dream up those Fantasy Land goals

When I'm working with my clients on leaning into your instincts and forging your path forwards I like to start with a reflection or journalling prompt. The aim is to journal about your dream life, imagining there are no limits, no 'proven' pathways and no one right way to get there. This is all about dreaming up those Fantasy Land goals.

This is a fun activity where you get to dream as big as you like and cherry-pick exactly those outcomes, results and stories that represent true success to you. What comes up for you? Are you excited? Nervous?

When working through this, remove all expectations from others, society and what you think you *should* do and come back to YOUR version of success. The more detailed you are with your Fantasy Land goals, the more you can structure your business model around what it's going to take to make it all possible.

Once you have your Fantasy Land list, write down three clear action steps for each goal. Keep them handy, in further chapters we will dive into taking bold action toward them!

I know I've said it already, but I'll say it again and again because it's important to let it sink in. ANYTHING you want to achieve is possible. But first, you need to DECIDE what that is. The 'how' doesn't have to make logical sense right now for it to be possible. Remember, there's no single 'right' way to move forward. Your clothes aren't one size fits all, so neither should your business approach. There are something like 2,185,962 ways to achieve a goal, build a business and make money.

Key Insights

- When creating goals, people often set to achieve 'things' rather than outcomes – and we end up wasting time and energy – and our goals are no closer to being achieved.

- Make sure you are clear on your values, so you know exactly what your success metrics are, and you can then go after them.

- Without this clarity, it's way too easy to get caught up chasing metrics of success that don't matter to you.

- The whole purpose of your subconscious mind is to protect and help you, which can lead to accidental self-sabotage.

- Shifting your mindset and moving into Fantasy Land is where the real fun begins – and where the magic happens.

**The main reason why you don't
have the level of success and wealth
you want is because, at the subconscious
level, *you don't actually want it*.**

CHAPTER 4

How to Stop Self-sabotaging

Hi, my name is Jessica, and I'm a 'Nice Girl'.

Well, I was – I'm not anymore. For so long, I held onto the deepest belief that when I shine too bright or have too much success, it offends or upsets others. So, I dimmed my light for a long time.

This is a belief I held for many, many years. It began in school when I started buying into the idea (subconsciously) that to stand out would be a bad idea. I always achieved good grades at school and so did my best friend. But soon, I noticed a pattern. Whenever she aced a test, achieving higher marks than me, I was genuinely happy for her. She in turn would celebrate her 'win' over me *so loudly*. On the flip side, when it was my turn to hold the spotlight, she projected her disappointment onto me, and I really felt it.

We've all experienced people like this in our lives, whether it's when we're at school, at work, in our social lives or even within our family units. It's how we react to situations, the self-awareness that we bring, and the stories we tell ourselves that will create the belief. In this situation (and many more throughout my life),

I created a limiting belief that it wasn't safe for me to share my success. As a result, one of my biggest shadows has been playing the role of the 'Nice Girl'. The alternative, in my view, was to be the bitch, bossy, greedy, arrogant – none of which sounds too nice, does it? Why would I want to be any of these?

When I am too successful, it upsets others and that creates a 'success shadow'.

By being the nice girl, I played small and as a result I minimised other people's expectations of me. I didn't have to hold others' projections that because of my success, I must be a bitch, greedy or arrogant. As a result, I lost sight of my power and how much impact I could have if only I was more direct, celebrated my successes, and my opinions and stood up for unstoppable Jess. I had a safety screen and if I didn't have to share my opinion fully, no one could disagree with me. It felt very safe, very secure, and very boring. How this played out in my day-to-day life may sound familiar to you. I would avoid the limelight. When something great happened in my business, I would downplay it. In fact, I downplayed everything.

As I mentioned, this all felt very safe. But it was also keeping me, my world, and my success very small. It meant I wasn't celebrating my wins or successes; I was dimming it all down, so I didn't offend others or be seen as greedy or arrogant or undeserving. The worst part? Most of the time I didn't even realise I was doing it. And maybe you're doing it too? You might think this was due to a lack of confidence. It wasn't. The truth is, I have always known what I was capable of, and my goals and dreams have always reflected my self-belief. But I was worried that by celebrating my successes, loudly and proudly, I was going to push people away both in business and my personal life, so I kept it to myself.

Many people talk about fear of failure, but when you are an ambitious powerhouse, it's more likely to be a fear of success that holds you back.

There are other fears, of course, and there are several ways you could be dimming your light and standing in your way of dreaming and playing bigger, like:

- Fear of failure.
- Fear of judgment.
- Fear of disappointing yourself or others.
- Fear of working too many hours.
- Fear of missing out on time with loved ones.
- Fear of becoming disconnected from your children.

These are all very valid and can play a role in holding you back. But in my experience, for most people, fear of success is the big disconnect.

Are you a 'Nice Girl' too?

So, let's check-in, where have you been dimming your light? Can you trace the timeline of when you started to turn the lights down low? Record your responses in your journal.

Do you feel like you don't want to try too hard or aim too high so you can avoid the embarrassment, the judgment or the 'failure' that might come with levelling up?

If the answer is yes, then it's likely you have a fear of success.

In many situations, we are much more comfortable being stuck where we are because we avoid success. I know, it doesn't make much logical sense: success is the one thing we all desire above all else, right? While your conscious mind is saying YES give me all the success, your subconscious is running the show, and it gains so many benefits from keeping you playing small.

When you DON'T have success:

- You can remain relatable – likeable, down to earth.
- You get to avoid others' expectations of you because with more success comes higher standards.
- You get to avoid others' judgments of you and haters projecting their jealousy onto you.

There are higher stakes that come with holding larger levels of wealth and success. And without those huge levels of success, you can avoid the responsibility that comes with it. The list goes on! You're not going to play in Fantasy Land or allow yourself to dream bigger if it feels unsafe to you at a subconscious level. I've worked with entrepreneurs on addressing this exact issue and the realisation for them has been life changing.

To call in a whole new level of success, it first needs to feel like the safest place for us, otherwise we will keep coming up against self-sabotage.

Emma, a highly motivated and successful business owner was sabotaging her business success, it was all there in front of her she just needed to reach out and take it. Emma owned a very successful marketing agency, and her story is a powerful example of how finding that subconscious trigger that is holding you back can be a business game changer. This is her story:

> When Emma and I started working together, she created huge amounts of success over a very short time. Within three months she had tripled her revenue. Emma had moved away from clients paying her at most $1000 to $10,000-plus. She felt on top of the world.
>
> Soon after, Emma started to hit a wall. She began procrastinating, sales felt hard and then her income started to dip. She was met with rejection after rejection. It made no logical sense: the strategies, business model and marketing were all in place. So, what happened?
>
> We dug into her fears around success and the stories she was holding in her subconscious. In the past, she had run a different business, and at the peak of her success, a close friend had betrayed her and went out of her way to hurt my client. We're talking sabotaging deals and interfering with clients; gossiping and turning her friends against her; the works.
>
> Ultimately, the toxicity of the environment and the blows to her past business and her self-confidence led Emma to shut down that business. She felt abandoned, she was a failure, and the story or belief she had created around that experience was powerful in its depth and impact: 'When I am successful, it is painful and the people I love abandon me.' That's a BIG reason to want to avoid success, right?
>
> Once we drilled down and discovered the impact of this part of her business life, it all made sense – her procrastination, her lack of follow up, her difficulty chasing leads. This was the reason she was self-sabotaging. Funnily enough, it wasn't until we dug into

her past that she even remembered this moment. It has all been sitting in her subconscious, firing off 'survival' mechanisms to make sure Emma never felt that way again. Her subconscious was sabotaging her success. She wasn't aware of the impact it was having on her current business and once we created the awareness, we were able to make some powerful mindset shifts.

In the same way Emma was unable to recognise that she was self-sabotaging her success, it also took me a long time to realise that by undermining my success, I was limiting myself and my results. These days, both Emma and I own our success. From my perspective, I flaunt that I am playing deep in Fantasy Land. I'm sure there are elements to Emma and my story that are familiar to you because growing up, whether it was family dynamics, siblings, or friends, we were taught to be the good girl, to not shine too brightly or stand out too much, be 'too much', or upset others by 'hogging' the attention.

The truth is, that having huge success is a mirror for others. They see in you their dreams, and if they realise they aren't playing in Fantasy Land while you are, that gets a reaction. It's uncomfortable for a lot of people. Sometimes, they will feel jealousy and resentment, especially when it appears to be easy. It can be difficult to believe success can be that easy and they will try to pick the holes in what you've achieved, so they can feel better about where they are at. And that's okay – they're also on their journey.

But hear me when I say, you do not have to dull your shine or success to make others more comfortable with where they are at. I believe the more we do the uncomfortable thing and shine, the more it raises the collective standard and shows others what is truly possible. This is your big old permission slip to enter your obnoxiously successful era and own it!

I have also learnt that haters will be part of your reality no matter what you do, how hard you try to be liked, or how real your success is. I've found that as I embraced my success, I have also opened up to being on the receiving end of more projections, negativity and expectations.

In the past, if someone had written a less-than-positive social media post about me or had made a negative comment directed my way or in a group, I would have been sent on an emotional spiral. But as I began owning the parts of me that could also be a bitch, arrogant, greedy, or any of the other traits we reject within ourselves, I began to understand that all this negativity comes from a place of hurt and projection and the hate began to hurt less.

The bottom line: this is your life, own it

If you want to be truly successful and achieve results that you can only imagine in your wildest dreams, you need to accept that this comes with a flip side.

Haters are going to pop out of the woodwork:

- No matter how hard you hide your success.
- No matter what you outwardly say or do.
- No matter what effort you go to downplay your wins.
- No matter how much energy and focus you invest into them.
- No matter how nice, kind, caring and supportive you are.

Even if you are the nicest person in the world – haters are still going to come for you. It is impossible to please everyone, and this is okay. More importantly, pleasing people is not your goal – especially if it's the reason why you block your success.

It's time to own it, own your success, your light, your opinions, all of it!

Start to notice the moments where you begin to dim your light and actively choose to shine bright.

Be Aware of Your Beliefs and Shadows

Have you ever set yourself a really big goal, but no matter how hard you try, no matter what you throw at it or how much you really want to achieve it, you keep falling short? Did you find yourself trapped in a relentless cycle of procrastination where regardless of your efforts, breaking free seemed like an elusive goal?

When this happens, you can end up feeling stagnant. Say you keep hitting the same monthly revenue over and over and there's no growth, or perhaps you see a change, but it's simply not enough to meaningfully shift how you feel and enable you to create those next levels of success and ease.

It's like this invisible ceiling you keep coming up against. You know HOW to take action. You could increase your prices, post on social media, take the next steps. But for some reason, knowing the next action to take seems like the hardest thing in the world, and so you avoid doing it. Understand that there's a deeper subconscious reason *why* you can't make the changes you so badly want. Yes, sometimes we just need to pull up our big girl panties and do the damn thing, but we can also look a little deeper and be curious about why these patterns show up.

As we've discussed we all have subconscious thoughts, opinions and beliefs that shape the way we think about ourselves and the world around us. If these beliefs are left unchecked, they can have a significant impact on your success. If you believe something negative about yourself, your potential, or your ability to achieve your dreams, you'll keep hitting the same roadblocks repeatedly until you change your beliefs.

When you aren't aware of how you are creating your reality, it shows up as self-sabotage.

You begin procrastinating, overthinking what to say and how to show up, and you may feel overwhelmed, anxious, or just avoid things altogether. We've all felt these things from time to time, right? But when there is a recurring pattern, it's time to dig deeper!

Fact: we know that it is extremely difficult to undertake change when our subconscious mind runs the show. It's so much easier to continue to work on autopilot. We also know that when we bring CONSCIOUS awareness to these roadblocks, that's when we can change them.

The goal of our subconscious mind is to keep us safe. The disconnection arises when we realise that to scale our business, we need to embrace discomfort and really lean into feeling uncomfortable.

So, to start attracting *more* into your life and business, you need to make a conscious move to shift the deep beliefs you are still holding on to – otherwise, it will continue to play out in your subconscious, and you won't even realise. The first step in this process is to understand what shadows and limiting beliefs are. Often, people teach limiting beliefs and shadow work very separately, but I believe they are very much connected.

Shadows are the parts of us that we have unconsciously rejected from our concept of self. Shadow work is about shining a bright light, illuminating the blind spot within our psyche and understanding why we rejected the aspects that challenged the carefully crafted image we have of ourselves.

Shadows are like an eraser, scrubbing out the traits we don't like. We are all born with the potential of every trait: bitchiness, arrogance, honesty and more. But as we go through life, we learn that some of these traits are 'unlikeable', and they detract from who we want to be. So, we ignore them, erasing them from our personalities. But they never truly disappear; they are a part of our subconscious.

Keep in mind that shadows may be dark, but they are not the ugly part of you. They can even have lighter aspects, such as power or confidence, even playfulness. You don't get rid of shadows; you integrate them. To do that, you need to let go of the shame and guilt, you can't integrate traits you feel shameful about.

A limiting belief is an underlying unconscious story or rule we have created based on the experience to keep us safe and the shadow hidden. A limiting decision is a decision you made and then continued to make until it turned into a belief.

Many of our beliefs are formed when we're young when our subconscious mind is more impressionable, and we then carry it throughout our lives. Now not all our beliefs are negative, I mean you've made it this far on your entrepreneurial journey, so you have some real positives in your toolkit. However, if you've attached your self-worth to a limiting belief, it can wreak havoc (until you work through it).

For instance, let's say as a child, you were very assertive and confident. You were the type of kid who knows what they want and isn't afraid to ask for it. But this attitude wasn't received well by adults, and you were told off by teachers and bullied for being so forthright. You began to feel embarrassment and shame, so you stayed safe, hiding away the parts of you that identify with being assertive, bitchy and bold. This manifests into a 'bitch' shadow and gets hidden deeper and deeper in the subconscious.

Your limiting belief creates a story that says: 'When I share my opinions or ask for what I want, people think I am a bitch.' As you get older, you learn to stay small, quiet, and hidden. These beliefs become a defence mechanism to protect you from negative outcomes like anxiety, imposter syndrome, conflict or being judged. But the truth is, they limit you from your full potential.

We *all* have subconscious blocks that stop us from achieving our dreams or even our everyday goals. To identify and change these beliefs, you need to work on your self-awareness muscle. The secret to conquering this is being accountable and taking responsibility for the beliefs you have created for yourself.

How to Get Out of Your Own Way

If you desire one thing, and you know you really, really want it: that's great. But your desire isn't the problem.

The main reason you still don't have the level of success and wealth you want is because, at the subconscious level, *you don't actually want it.*

Ouch, right? I know what you're thinking. *Of course,* you want to be successful. *Of course,* you want to be wealthy. So how could I possibly suggest the reason you don't want this high-level success is ... you?

Here's the thing: you're not going to play in Fantasy Land or allow yourself to dream bigger if at a subconscious level it feels unsafe. No change means no judgment, no responsibility, no burnout, and no risk of failure. And it also means no growth. As we explored in the last chapter, there's a reason why it is hard to change things when our subconscious mind runs the show. Running on autopilot is easy and safe, which is why (without realising it) we can procrastinate until it is too late. The good news is our minds have neuroplasticity, meaning we can mould and change them – it's not carved in stone.

Being honest with yourself is the most uncomfortable work you will do as an entrepreneur.

It's scary to look inward; you never know what you will find. But the freedom and HUGE levels of success you desire are waiting on the other side. Rewiring the mind is a lifelong journey and we will forever be discovering new things about ourselves.

You are already worthy and capable of claiming all the limitless success you desire. But to unlock that potential, it is a *process*. The process of unlearning everything you thought you 'should' be or do, and instead, energetically, and intuitively take the action that creates the abundance you want to see, feel and have. That process begins here:

Step 1. Notice your patterns
Looking at patterns in your behaviour, thoughts and responses to situations can help you spot a shadow or block. Do you feel triggered, fearful, or resistant toward certain activities or actions?

Identify the tasks, the events, the situations that you are procrastinating about, the ones that you know are key to achieving your goals. Some of the common patterns could include:

- You're a people pleaser, so you keep offering people discounts or over-explaining yourself and your services.
- You're scared of putting yourself out there, so you shy away from social media or self-promotion.
- You feel the need to over-explain yourself and prove your worth.
- You keep attracting intense, high-needs clients who create equally intense levels of stress, because you cannot turn down work (even when you know it's not a good client fit).
- You don't share or celebrate your success loudly even though you wish you did.
- You keep running out of money, or you hit the same revenue number each month, no matter what you do.
- No matter how hard you try to finish work earlier, you're still at your desk late at night.
- You know *exactly* what you need to do to create more success but keep procrastinating and avoiding it like the plague. An example of this is selling. Many business owners find it difficult to promote their offers because it feels unapproachable or difficult.

We continue to play out patterns because our subconscious needs are met. We are very intelligent humans – nothing is by accident. But without risk, we can never have our Fantasy Level success.

Notice your patterns to uncover deeper self-sabotage

Ask yourself:

What patterns are showing up in my life?

What do I currently claim to hate or want to stop doing? Yet I keep doing it?

What challenges continue to show up?

Grab a pen and journal to answer the questions.

Step 2. Consider the unconscious gain

This is when your subconscious gains something from staying stuck. Remember, our subconscious loves predictability and keeping you safe so it acts in what it thinks is your best interest, which sometimes may contradict your goals.

Unearthing the underlying benefits your subconscious gains is the key to achieving awareness and shifting the behaviour at the core. They could include:

- Constantly discounting – benefit: you feel liked and appreciated by the client receiving the discount and avoid feeling greedy. Or it gives you a fallback if you don't deliver 100% for your client ('well what do they expect, I gave them a deal they can't expect perfection.')
- You water down your opinions – benefit: you can avoid being seen as a bitch.
- You don't share or celebrate your success loudly – benefit: people won't think you're arrogant or greedy.

- Accepting every client who knocks on your door even if the reality of saying 'yes' means 70-hour working weeks and toxic client relationships – benefit: makes you feel busy, in demand and successful.
- Keep hitting the same revenue cap no matter what you do – benefit: you're not having to fully see your power or have expectations from others for you to perform.
- You continue to work long hours – benefit: you feel more worthy of success when the journey has been a hard, uphill hustle.

What is your subconscious gaining by keeping you stuck?

Ask yourself:

Why do these patterns keep showing up? What am I gaining from these substandard results?

What do I subconsciously gain by being or doing the things I say I hate?

What are all the benefits my subconscious is gaining?

Write your reflections in your journal.

Vanessa, a smart and ambitious video content creator, was capping her income limit. She procrastinated on acting on her big goals and she couldn't understand why. This is her story:

Initially, when I asked Vanessa what her subconscious had to gain from keeping her 'stuck', she replied 'I'm not gaining anything', which is a very logical answer. Vanessa had a goal to increase her income, so what would she gain by not working towards it?

When you start to do this work, you need to think like your illogical subconscious mind, which as we know is gaining *real* satisfaction from keeping you safe. Vanessa and I dug deep to unpack *why* this was showing up and subsequently capping her success.

Vanessa was holding a subconscious belief created in her past work life in which earning more money equalled overwork and running herself into the ground. She had been earning a great wage, but was overloaded and struggling; her mental health had suffered. Not surprisingly this solidified her subconscious belief that more money equals burnout.

Think about this: if Vanessa's subconscious was holding onto that belief as if it were the absolute truth (and let's face it there was hard evidence from past experiences), then why would it allow her to power through and create overflowing income and success in her business, *if* it was going to harm her? It simply wouldn't. Our subconscious is operating on autopilot in the background in ways we don't often realise. That is why she needed to identify the subconscious blocks to unlock more ease and flow on her journey to success.

Just pushing harder or being more motivated is not going to help if we hold onto a limiting belief.

Step 3. Integrate the changes

Awareness alone will begin to shift so much, but the next step in creating our new reality requires you to take action. You have two choices in life: to continue to play out the pattern or to choose a new path. Integration is where we acknowledge the shadows and limiting beliefs and transform those into healthy tools instead. When you integrate your shadows into yourself and your business, this acceptance becomes your superpower.

So, this might look like: If you have an arrogance shadow and you don't celebrate your wins, due to the fear of being seen as arrogant and bragging, integrating it in a healthy way could mean no longer watering yourself down on social media and sharing your wins loudly. By doing this, people *could* potentially see you as arrogant (and that's okay). When we accept the parts of ourselves that we have rejected, it creates a level of safety in our subconscious to hold people's judgment if they do see you as arrogant.

Or if you are constantly discounting your products so you feel appreciated and validated (from others), where can you appreciate and validate yourself more? This personal validation will heavily reduce the desire to constantly discount because you will be so grounded in your self-worth.

Vanessa was able to create sustainable business practices that supported her mental health and removed her fear of burnout (instead of just trying to push for more sales). She worked on creating a new belief: 'I am capable of creating major levels of success and wealth and my health and wellbeing are thriving'. Then, she journalled on all the evidence and proof that this was true. This process moved her shadows and beliefs to a positive, accommodating place.

Create your new reality

Ask yourself:

> What behaviour do I need to clean up or stop doing? Example: No longer discounting or overexplaining yourself or showing up in the way you feel called to.

> What new intention can I set to create a new narrative?

> Look for all the evidence and proof: where in the past have you proven your shadow or limiting beliefs wrong? Start to build a case for your subconscious to create a new belief.

Record your responses in your journal and refer to these on your journey to creating a new belief.

One final word on this: it's not an overnight process.

This is a big action with a big opportunity – almost a lifelong journey – and the discovery and growth behind doing this work is not a task we just tick off our list and then we're all set. We will *always* be able to dig deeper and become even more congruent. But to start with, choose one area to focus on and work through unearthing and resolving. A whole level will shift with this extra awareness, and small changes over time lead to big, meaningful, life-altering new realities.

Key Insights

- We each develop beliefs that keep us safe, but they hold us back from our big goals.

- The main reason why you don't have the level of success and wealth you want is because, at the subconscious level, you don't want it.

- Shadows are the parts of ourselves that we have rejected from our concept of self and are unconscious.

- A limiting belief is an underlying subconscious story or rule we have created for ourselves, based on experience, that keeps us safe and hides the shadow.

- Connecting with your shadow self and overcoming your limiting beliefs is crucial for your growth and success.

I love discomfort, I get so excited because I know what's on the other side.

CHAPTER 5

How to Stop Playing Small

Step into Fantasy Land with me for a moment. I want you to imagine something ... If you knew your goals were GUARANTEED, what would you aim for? If you knew there was NO WAY to fail, what action would you take?

I've covered my concept of Fantasy Land and how to dream bigger, achieve bigger and generally step into a bigger life, but the truth is, you can't play in Fantasy Land unless you are taking massive bold action. To do this, you need to stop playing small. So, in this chapter, I'm going to unpack my ethos and principles of playing a bigger game – along with my proven techniques and strategies to help you get there.

For me, I've never been a 'bare minimum' kind of girl. I'm more of a 'balls deep, hell for leather, give it everything I've got' type. I wouldn't describe myself as someone who plays small. And still, I find myself having breakthroughs around my mindset and finding areas where I've been limiting myself.

When I notice myself starting to get comfortable, I shake it up again and again, because every time I meet myself at new edges, it becomes my new normal.

Growth is my biggest value and stepping outside of my comfort zone has always felt like the safest place for me to be. And I want the same for you, but I know this is something a lot of people struggle with. When working with my clients, I often hear fears like:

- I just don't know if it'll work out.
- It's a lot of money to invest – what if it doesn't pay off?
- What if I take a big risk and it fails?

You get the gist. While the fears and anxieties can be different, they all have one thing in common: they're playing small, 'just to be safe'.

This type of thinking might keep you safe, it does after all prevent you from making big decisions and taking huge leaps, which could be risky. But it also keeps you small, limits your success and your growth, and stops you from reaching your true potential.

There are two types of frequency you can operate from. One is: 'I don't know if it'll work out' so you play it smaller than you'd like to 'just to be safe'. The other is: 'My next level goals are INEVITABLE' and you make bold moves accordingly because of course you would. They're worlds apart and the frequency that you choose is always the results you will get.

The keyword here is 'choosing'. You get to choose, in this moment, how things play out for you. If you knew your goals were guaranteed, how would you be taking action? What moves would you be making? Because guess what until you decide your goals are GUARANTEED, they are not going to land in your lap.

Deciding your goals are guaranteed

Imagine your goals for a moment. Now imagine there are two versions of you; one who is *unsure* if it will work out – what moves are you making? What actions are you committing (or not committing) to?

The other version of you is so *convinced that it's already yours* (cue Jess at age 12, where my level of delusional thinking had me ready to buy an investment property). How are you showing up? When do you believe that a positive outcome is absolutely guaranteed?

Journal on this and see what comes up for you, because often, we know what we should be doing but there is some resistance towards taking action because we are not 100% sure yet.

- Where are you still playing small?
- And how can you level up and play a much bigger, more abundant, more profitable, and more successful game?

It's yours to decide, right now, at this moment – it's time to play BIGGER.

Life is Not a Practice Run

Here are my principles for taking massive, bold action: There is no rehearsal for life. So why are you practising? I can't tell you how many times I've heard people ask if they can 'just practise' with their business:

- Can I try it out on a smaller scale first?
- What if I just do a soft launch to test it out?

- Do you think I should wait until I'm more confident to start charging my correct price?
- Can I juggle my day job until my business revenue grows? (Spoiler: unless you have a *really* clear goal here, a scarcity mindset can keep you stuck in this job or business dynamic forever.)

Insert any narrative you might be currently telling yourself that means you are not yet going *all in* on your big goals – be honest.

It's like adding way too much water to your cordial. It dilutes the result and isn't anywhere near as good as it could be. And here's the bottom line: if you stay in this 'practice mindset', you're setting yourself up to play small. And it's limiting you and your results too.

Do you sometimes wish there was a fast-forward button to get to your goals? Well, this is it. Instead of 'practising' and spending time, energy and likely money on something that you don't *really* want. What if you could instead take a massive leap, go all in, and be living your dream life and achieving all your wildest goals sooner?

I guess since you are reading this, that you already know you are capable of full-scale dreamy success, but you're not allowing yourself to play at that level yet. Let's change that! If there is one piece of advice I can give you, it's this handy little hack. *Act like you are already there.* Like you're already 100% nailing it. Like you've already accomplished your goals, and you're rolling in clients and revenue, and you're so confident that your results are guaranteed, you radiate the energy of S U C C E S S.

I get it, it's easy to have this Big Boss energy when things are going well for you. It's harder when things aren't so rosy. But that's the *real* test. Remember, when I shared my rock bottom story – when I didn't even have a few dollars left in my bank to pay for parking, yet I still showed up and moved forward? I went all in, there was no warm-up, and there was no practice run for me.

It's all about having deep self-trust and faith in yourself and what you can achieve. And sometimes, you need to take those big leaps in pursuit of the longer-term, bigger vision.

When you go all in, take bigger risks and leap before you're ready you'll have to be okay with falling over sometimes, and potentially skinning your knees along the way, it's all part of the journey.

------ ⚡ ------

No more practising!

Ask yourself and journal your responses:
  What am I afraid of or waiting for?
  What is the worst that could happen? Often, it's not really all that bad, and there's a simple fix.
  What action would I take right now, if I was playing big and went all in on my goals?
  If you want to dream big; if you want your business to be global; if you want it to be a success, then you have to decide that there is no more 'practising'. It's time to back yourself and take that leap!

Move Fast, Fail Fast – Succeed Even Faster

The most successful people in the world say that the key to success is making a decision. Seems simple, right? The point is making any decision is better than no decision at all. Even making no decision, is a decision – even if it is to remain stuck where you are.

This is a life mantra I live and breathe. Making slow decisions is the fastest route to being overwhelmed and burnt out. At its simplest: every decision you hold onto takes up energetic space in your mind and the more you delay taking action, the more you practise, overthink, doubt yourself and sit in indecision. I truly believe the number one reason why I've created so much success in my business is because I move so fast. I certainly didn't create these kinds of epic results by moving slow.

When I started my coaching business, I had the idea to launch a membership as my first offering. I hadn't stepped out the exact plan of how I wanted to run it, the name, or the nitty gritty details, but I knew I needed to take the leap and go all in right then and there. All I needed to start was a basic website and a way for clients to sign up and pay. So, I decided on a name (which I later ended up changing), chose the platform I would run my sessions through (Facebook groups were the easiest platform at the time) and set to work on building that website.

Within two hours, I had a website and payment system set up, I had posted to social media and on that first day 12 people joined. Yep, from 'I should do this' to my website being live and people paying me within just 120 minutes. How? Because it was by no means perfect, but it was a start – and done is better than perfect.

When I first launched my podcast, I didn't spend hours

researching the best microphones, or googling how to start a podcast, or looking at what everyone else was doing on their podcast to try and gain inspiration. Instead, that very same day, I recorded the first episode on my phone, took a self-timer photo (again on the iPhone) for the cover art, made a basic logo with a font I liked and set it to 'live'.

In less than 24 hours, I was a podcaster. Without a doubt, I had work to complete, promotion to activate and exposure to create but it was 'done', I was 'out there', and I had a podcast to develop and work on. A real podcast that needed a real commitment. Instead of obsessing over the right or wrong way to do it, trying to be a perfectionist, or just letting fears or imposter syndrome stop me, I just took the leap. Over time I have re-created the artwork, changed the name of the podcast, and definitely invested in state-of-the-art microphones, but I didn't *need* any of that to start.

You may be telling yourself all the reasons why you need to wait or spending all your time on planning when the most important part is just doing the damn thing and figuring it out along the way.

There are many more examples of when I, or my clients, moved fast and then pivoted, adapted and evolved decisions. If you want to achieve your goals sooner, you need to start making fast (and informed) decisions, too. If I had waited until I had all my tech requirements, strategy, and a complete plan, it could have been weeks or months before I even launched my podcast. Instead by dreaming big, and going after my podcasting goals, I had weeks and months of experience, listeners, and audience growth.

The key to success is to leap before you are really ready

Ask yourself:

> What do I need to do, to move one (or ten) steps closer to my goals TODAY. Not tomorrow. Journal your answer and then go and do it, NOW.

Some of my tips to lean into this way of working include:

- Making decisions from a place of empowerment – not from scarcity or fear.
- Getting out of your head and stop over thinking; you already know what the right next move is for you, so find out what is blocking you from taking the next step.
- Accepting that the perfect time doesn't exist.
- Taking action before you're READY. Act when the opportunity is in front of you, not when you're ready – it might not exist by the time you feel more comfortable diving in.
- Knowing that your next level will always feel a little scary, but true growth and success comes from feeling the fear and doing it anyway.

If There's a Will, There's Always a Way, Just Watch Me

If you take just one thing from this chapter – hell if you take just one thing from this entire book – I hope, it's this. Because it has the power to transform your life. And it's this:

Never. Take. No. For. An. Answer.

If I accepted all the 'noes' I've heard in my time, I straight up wouldn't have the life I have today. If I *didn't* push back and look for another way to move forward whenever a door was slammed shut in my face, I'd still be:

- Working long hours for someone else instead of choosing my own schedule.
- Earning a tenth of what I earn today, without the potential for limitless growth.
- Wasting my mornings in a long commute instead of starting my mornings at the beach.
- And just generally living a miserable life, instead of living with ease, flow, and wealth.

Real talk: only *we* get to decide what we want. And only we get to step up and say: 'You know what? I AM doing this'. The power is all yours!

So how do you do this? How do you get out of your comfort zone and choose persistence and determination as your default settings? When discussing roadblocks, rejections, or challenges, I often say: it's not about something being impossible, it's about how willing you are to *make it happen* – read that again and let it sink in. If you get ten rejections in a row, do you decide no one wants to work with you and give up because it's hard or embarrassing? OR – do you continue to ask another 50 or more people until you get a yes? This applies to business and your personal pursuits too.

> **If you are willing enough to make it happen, there is always a way – it may not always be the easiest way, but a way, nevertheless. It's up to you to decide how willing you are to make it happen.**

There are so many moments, when the 'experts' have told me 'you can't do that', and I say, 'watch me'. When I set a major goal to have my story published in *Forbes*, leading press experts advised me that I needed to be in business for longer and have more skin in the game to even be considered. So, I set out and found the contacts myself, pitched my story – and ended up being featured in *Forbes* not just once, but three times.

When start-up queen Lisa Messenger planned her national tour and didn't add Perth to the itinerary, I campaigned to change her tour plans to include Western Australia (and I was determined to meet and learn from her, too; I organised the whole Perth event and ended up speaking on stage with her).

When I was seeking wholesale deals for my first business, I emailed over 5000 individual emails to buyers over an entire year, before I received a reply and a sizeable order.

When my builder told me it was going to be at least 12 months before they could even get started on the construction of my new house, I said 'no way'. They started building just a few months later.

When my beautiful engagement ring was deemed too delicate to be resized and I was informed should be worn as a pendant for the rest of my life, I said, 'no way'. Five jewellers later, I have a perfectly sized engagement ring sitting pretty on my finger (there was no way it was going to become a damn pendant).

It turns out that when you don't take no for an answer, a solution can always be found. Here are some strategies that if you choose to live by in your life and business, major things will begin to unlock for you:

- If you don't get a yes, ask more people. Ask different people. Ask questions differently. There's always a solution, sometimes you have to be creative to find it.

- Remind yourself: who said you can't? Anyone who is standing in your way and saying no is just a challenge for you to dream bigger, do better and take real action.
- First you need to *decide* what you want the outcome to be, then try every route until it becomes your reality. Don't leave it up to chance – this one is key when entering any negotiation, business deal or pitch.
- Take ownership and know that *you* have control of how your unlimited growth plays out. Once you stop blaming external factors (other people, 'rules', money, lack of results) a weight is lifted, because you realise that true success is within reach.
- You need to pave your own path. You don't need to follow the directions of how people have done it before – true innovators will find their own way to go under it, over it, through it and around it to get to where they want to go.

Save these techniques and refer to them as often as you can. Then send me a message when you land some epic deals and make that shit happen because I want to celebrate with you (and I already know you're about to make some wild things happen, so I'll be waiting).

Bare Minimum Input Equals Bare Minimum Results

You can't expect massive, game-changing, out of this world success and still show up with bare minimum energy.

To be 100% crystal clear, I am not a fan of hustle culture. I don't believe you need to go above and beyond, burning yourself out working 100 hours a week and over delivering to get big results in your business. I'm all about creating ease, freedom, and flow in business. But and this is important, when you are putting energy into your business, you need to be all in.

Slapping up a single story on social media with dot points about your offer every day means yeah, technically, you are 'selling', but it's coming from a place of bare minimum energy. I can guarantee your audience can feel it and are not going to be motivated to take action. Or maybe you're spending hours scrolling and consuming other people's content, comparing and overthinking, and you call it 'research'? You then have zero energy left to create your content and as a result bare minimum energy in communicating with your audience – the very reason you were 'researching' to start with. And you wonder why you're not gaining any new followers or clients?

Being smart with your energy is how you create massive success, without burning out or making life sacrifices. It comes from a place of strategically knowing where to put your energy (and where not to) and being intentional about how you create results and impact in your world. This is how I create massive results in my business and make time to go to the beach or relax. Everything I do, I do it with intention.

In your own life and business, try this: instead of pursuing a *lot* of things with 10% energy for each, choose to take on a few key elements with 100% energy. Then, when you show up for your clients, on social media and for yourself, you do so with purpose and a deeper understanding of the outcome you want to achieve.

Be intentional with your energy

Ask yourself:

> What are the few, key steps I need to take to get me closer to my goals today?
>
> Write these in your journal.
>
> Then, do those things with 100% energy and attention and forget about the rest.
>
> Watch how fast things begin to shift for you when you lean into this.

Turn the Dial up a Notch

It's easy to become frustrated when we feel like we're constantly putting the work in, promoting ourselves, creating opportunities and reaching out to our community, and yet no one seems to be buying. But how much are you *actually* doing?

Many of us tend to *overestimate* the amount of work we are *actually* doing, especially when it comes to selling and marketing our offer, our business, and our brand. In navigating the spotlight, it can feel as though all eyes are on you. To safeguard you, your mind compensates by embellishing your workload and effort, creating the perception of a more significant task than you've undertaken. To understand why your mind is sabotaging your results you need to dive into the facts and figures. You could start by checking your marketing activities and archives.

Instead of taking our mind's word for it, we need to gain visibility around the hard facts.

One of my coaching clients was disappointed with her results and was feeling a little deflated. I prompted her to check her social media and marketing platform activity. That's when she realised that over the past two weeks, she'd reached out to her community with her offer a total of ... wait for it ... once. Her mind was blown, but you can't argue with the facts. With a new fire lit under her, and equipped with key sales strategies we developed, she doubled down on her marketing efforts and within 24 hours, generated three new enquiries.

It's not uncommon that we try to overcomplicate the path to success, look for new strategies or just do 'more', when in fact, achieving massive and fast results can be as simple as doubling down on the proven strategies we are already implementing. As we know by now, our brains can deceive us (especially when we are overthinking everything) – so check your stats, instead of relying solely on your memory. And turn that dial up a notch.

Comparison is Your Biggest Expander

You've likely felt it at some point along your journey, that feeling of envy or jealousy when you find out someone has achieved something you wanted. You start thinking all sorts of things, like:

- Why them, not me?
- What did they do to achieve that?
- How did they pull that off?

It's an uncomfortable feeling that we usually try to avoid. But I believe we have the perception of comparison all wrong.

Firstly, when you become intent and clear on your version of success and become focused on paving your path in true alignment with who you are and what you want to achieve, comparison won't even be on your radar. But here's the deal if you do feel it creeping in – it's a gift.

Often the advice is to try and rationalise the success of others. We hear comments like: 'Well, you don't know how well they're *actually* doing.' In other words: let's assume they must be unhappy in other areas of their life, because no one can be successful, wealthy, happy, healthy, and blessed, right?! It fuels the narrative that wild levels of success, happiness, health, and all the good stuff are not possible for anyone, including ourselves.

This whole approach of minimising or being derogatory about successful competitors, peers, and fellow entrepreneurs never made sense to me. I don't want to 'put anyone down'. Instead, I'd rather see someone kicking goals and use it as an opportunity to be inspired to step up and live to my full potential. It's proof of what is possible. That's why I see comparison as the biggest expander.

It has also been suggested that unfollowing or blocking someone who triggers these feelings of comparison and inadequacy will somehow make us feel bigger, better and smarter. The truth is, there is a reason why we're triggered by someone else's success. We can block one person or many, but the issue is still going to be there. They're a mirror reflecting our success, perhaps reminding us that we are still playing small. And that's uncomfortable, right?

If we didn't believe that we could achieve the same level of success as the person we're comparing ourselves to, we wouldn't be triggered by it. We don't walk around being triggered by Oprah every day, because we likely don't see her on our level (yet – it's coming).

It's not surprising that when we see someone achieving goals, the same goals we believe *are* within our reach, we become more aware of our own limitations and potential. Now this could be because you are playing smaller than you know you're capable of and that's a hard truth to accept. So instead of trying to rationalise someone else's success or avoiding them altogether, use these feelings of comparison as a big, fat catalyst to push yourself further and reach your own full potential.

Shake That Shit Up

Feeling comfortable? Okay great, but you know what I'm going to say next. That's the best time to shake that shit up and push yourself to new limits. When things begin to feel comfortable, it's because what once was your next level, is now your new normal.

This is a process I recently went through myself (and continually do). I noticed that I started to feel very comfortable with where I was, my business was growing, and it felt easier than ever. So, I knew it was time to audit my business and shake things up.

I decided to review my pricing and make some big changes and increases. At first, I'll admit, I went a little bit into a scarcity mindset (this increase was a big one because I love pushing new limits and challenging myself): *what if no one buys at this price?* The opportunity in these moments is expanded. This is the best time to gain insights into our Fantasy Land goals, and I realised that this was my opportunity to lean into where my next edges are and expand even further.

Get out of your comfort zone

This is my challenge to you. Look at your business and ask yourself:

Are you feeling truly fulfilled and expanding?

Or are you comfortable (or worse – just going through the motions)?

Here are a few questions to challenge yourself and shake things up:

- What areas can you revisit to expand?
- What parts of your business are screaming out for attention?
- What areas of your business could you reinvent?

Reflect on the questions and write your answers in your journal.

Examine at all the areas in your business and look for those comfort zones: marketing, sales, prices, clients, offers, all of it. Then make some changes. It might be intimidating initially, but believe me, it's where the magic happens – and the Fantasy Land goals come to life.

This is your shake up call! Let's all push ourselves to expand and grow beyond what feels comfortable right now.

I love discomfort, I get so excited because I know what's on the other side. Remember: Whenever you begin to feel uncomfortable, it's because the 'next level you' hasn't fully landed yet, but she's coming.

You Don't Find Opportunities – You Make Them

I've noticed that a lot of people tend to wait for opportunities. They're excited about the potential and they're inviting those opportunities in – but they don't leave the waiting room and head out to *make it happen*.

Do you think the world's most successful people reach their goals because they get 'approached'? Because they sit there and twiddle their thumbs, thinking:

- I'm just going to wait until someone discovers me.
- I'm going to wait until I'm invited to be featured in the press.
- I'm going to wait to be invited on podcasts and to do media interviews.
- I'm going to wait until that major brand recognises how amazing I am and reaches out with a big contract to work together.

The biggest and most powerful action we can do in our business, and the main trait that I've seen in successful people (and something I've always done myself), is to:

Make It Happen.

By this I mean: I've created every single opportunity I've had. None of them have fallen in my lap. They've been the result of targeted ideas, energy and action on my behalf. I've learnt that if you want to create a result, you need to get out there and make it happen!

That's exactly how I pitched to and ended up with insanely talented, internationally renowned guests on my podcast. I make a list at the start of every year and then I'm tenacious about tracking them down and inviting them to speak to my audience (stalker vibes but make it cute).

I wouldn't have been featured in *Forbes* multiple times, landed major sponsorship deals, collaborated with the world's top brands, or secured dream clients in my highest paid offers. And let's be real, I don't always get what I want (I mean, Kris Jenner is still on my list) but you would be surprised to discover who says 'yes' if you're willing to put yourself out there and *ask*.

The next level

As you transition your thinking into playing a much bigger game, journal on some of these thought-starters to unlock that next level – the only way to start seeing major results flowing in, is to do the work:

Move Fast, Fail Fast, Succeed Even Faster

- When an opportunity knocks, is your first reaction to say 'yes' regardless of whether you feel confident about it or not?
- Are you willing to take action before you're ready – or are you still waiting for the perfect timing to step into your true power?

Repeat After Me: If There's a Will, there's a Way, Just Watch Me

- Have you tried all possible avenues and asked every single person you can, to get to a 'yes'?
- Have you taken ownership of your story and success? Remember, when you wait on others for validation or approval, you're giving your power away.

Bare Minimum Input Equals Bare Minimum Results

- Are you genuinely putting 100% energy into the needle-moving tasks in your business?
- Or are you spending 10% energy across a multitude of tasks that may have less impact on your results??

Turn the Dial Up a Notch

- Are you doing absolutely everything you can to promote your business, reach out to your community and make an impact in this world?

Comparison is Your Biggest Expander

- You have the choice to see comparison as an opportunity to be inspired to step up and live up to your full potential.
- Can you use any feelings of comparison as inspiration to push yourself further and reach your own full potential?

Shake that Shit Up

- Are you feeling truly fulfilled and expanding in your business, and are you ready to push yourself to expand and grow beyond what feels comfortable right now?
- What areas of life or business need a complete shake up?
- Will you still be charging the same prices, taking on the same projects, and working with the same clients in the future – or do you see more for yourself?

You Don't Find Opportunities – You Make Them

- Have you made a list of big, bold, crazy goals? What action can you take *right now* to work towards achieving them?
- Are you willing to put yourself out there and ask for what you want – and most importantly, how can you stop waiting and start taking action to make it happen?

Key Insights

- Until you decide your goals are GUARANTEED, they are not going to land in your lap.

- Making decisions fast is the key to reducing being overwhelmed and burnout. Every decision you hold onto takes up an energetic space in your mind.

- If you are willing enough to make it happen, there is always a way – it may not always be the easiest way, but a way, nevertheless. It's up to you to decide how willing you are to make it happen.

- Comparison won't even be on your radar when you become clear on your version of success and become focused on paving your path.

- Whenever you begin to feel uncomfortable, it's because the 'next level you' hasn't fully landed yet, but she's coming.

"
**Money is infinite in this world, and
I am claiming my piece.**

"

CHAPTER 6

Let's Get Real About Money

If there's one message that sticks with you from this chapter, I hope it's this: more money in the hands of a woman on a mission can only be a good thing.

I've already talked (a lot!) about success and how to work out what *truly* matters to you. But I wanted to give money its own chapter because it's So. Very. Complex. There is a taboo energy around the topic of money.

You may have felt it yourself when you saw the title of this chapter – some ingrained thoughts, beliefs or even subconscious triggers that prompted a reaction in you. This happens because when it comes to money:

- There are numerous conditioning and limiting beliefs we align money with.
- Many of these limiting beliefs we pick up in childhood.
- There is extensive unpacking we need to do so we can throw out what hasn't been working for us and embrace new, better, shinier ways to move forward.

This work is required at every level. You may be comfortable holding millions, but what about billions or even trillions? I know this can be powerful because I have changed my own life by going through this process. I have been on a huge journey when it comes to my mindset around money.

Remember when I had zero dollars to my name after five months into my first business? Jess from back then would go to every Pilates studio in town just to get the free trials because it felt 'too expensive' to sign up for a paid class. I would go to restaurants and choose what to eat based on the price, not what I wanted to eat.

When I travelled for work, I would cram a million meetings into one or two days because I didn't want to spend too much on accommodation. It would burn me out and I'd need two weeks to recover every single time. I kept those habits up, even when I started to earn more. My business wasn't creating as much income as it is now, but I had money.

These choices were not coming from a place of necessity, but from a place of not feeling worthy, not feeling wealthy and a huge place of scarcity mindset. It took a massive amount of personal work and growth to realise that *external* situations don't change how you feel *internally*. This work meant I was able to play in Fantasy Land and experience the ease and abundance of wild wealth, well before I was living it. Slowly but surely, I began building the proof that I am a wealthy and successful person.

For instance: I love Pilates. And it was a huge step into abundance for me when I decided to purchase my own Pilates reformer bed. I now have a calm and relaxing studio in my own home. I didn't 'wait until I was wealthy' to enjoy the benefits of wealth. Instead, I intentionally and proactively started surrounding myself with the proof of my abundance over time.

By making small changes like this, I sat in the energy of expansiveness and invited in even more wealth. My mission is to show more women that they can have huge levels of wealth, that it gets to feel easy and fun and can exceed their wildest dreams. You are already worthy and capable of creating these levels of wealth – the levels of overflowing abundance you've always dreamt of, and more.

Our perception of wealth, and the reality we therefore create around it, is all perspective and a construct of proximity. The closer we are to wealth and wealthy people or the more we experience it ourselves, the more realistic it becomes, and the more we normalise having large amounts of wealth for ourselves too.

Money flows in and flows out, just like an ocean tide. And just like the ocean, it's infinitely available and can be accessed by anyone.

When we can look at money in this way, everything changes. When you think of how much money exists in this world, you realise it flows between people, businesses and entities.

One great little hack I have for gaining proximity to crazy levels of wealth is reality TV. Hear me out! *The Real Housewives of Beverly Hills* is my favourite, and then *The Kardashians*, closely followed by *Bling Empire*. The levels of wealth on display in these shows are huge: I'm talking $5000 manicures, $50,000 sunglasses and 50 million-dollar homes. You really learn a lot from reality TV (some people call it trash TV, but all the smart girls are watching it!).

When watching these programs, I gain small moments of inspiration and motivation – they remind me, again and again, that there is *no limit* on how many people can be wealthy in the world. There's no finite list of millionaires, right? Some people have billions and billions of dollars, so why can't you?

At the end of the day, billionaires are just humans. The only difference between you and them is that they have said to themselves, 'I can have this kind of wealth'. Yes, some billionaires have grown up with generational wealth passed on to them, but there are plenty of self-made billionaires who started with nothing. If it's possible for them, it's possible for you too.

To claim what is already available to you, it takes shifting of inner beliefs (our inner world becomes our outer) and some simple planning and strategies. Why? Because many of us develop the limiting belief that 'rich people' are somehow separate from us and that obtaining large levels of wealth is 'not for me'. Or we might grow up with the belief that we shouldn't talk about money.

And let's not forget, so many people are mistakenly holding onto the belief that MORE WEALTH equals MORE WORK – so you actively avoid it. That can lead to a raft of subconscious core beliefs, like:

- I don't want to make more money because I don't want to work harder.
- I'm not capable of creating huge levels of wealth.
- I have never had money.
- I can't increase my prices – my clients won't pay more, or I will lose my clients.

- I have enough money; I don't need more.
- I can't charge people more; I just want to help.
- I don't want to make millions because I don't need all the problems that much money would bring.

We place a lot of energy around money, subconsciously or consciously, and I want to lift that for you, so you can invite major abundance and unlimited wealth into your life.

I firmly believe that more money in the hands of the right people is the gold standard, and I'm on a mission to help you crush *any* limiting beliefs you have about your earning potential.

Having more money allows you to:

- Decide what your schedule looks like each day.
- Choose the work you LOVE doing rather than having to make money from it.
- Remove the guilt or pressure to always be 'working' instead of living.
- Give to people and causes that mean the most to you.
- Have *choices* in life.

All sounds amazing, right? It's time for you to claim what is already available to you. Remember – you get to re-write your money story.

Say this out loud:

'I'm choosing to believe that money is infinite in this world, and I am claiming my piece today! I'm opting IN to the belief that money and wealth flow to me easily – without pushing, hustling, or sacrificing to get there – just purely enjoying the experience.'

Money is Not the Goal

Don't get me wrong – I'm all about setting big, huge, crazy financial goals and I want to inspire you to imagine what your life would be like if you made more money than you possibly know what to do with.

But I don't want you to move forward in your business with 'wealth' as your main motivator and goal. In fact, creating that kind of epic financial success all starts with the understanding that 'making money' is not the goal. Say what? Did I just have the audacity to say 'Making money isn't the goal' in a chapter that's all about making money?! I sure did – and here's why.

Success and wealth don't come about from 'chasing the money'.

Success and wealth are the result of you letting go of your ego and are created when you operate from a place of feeling confident, motivated, and lit up by what you do. That kind of energy is infectious and allows you to connect to your purpose. You're then 100% in alignment with the value you can offer and outcomes you can create for others – and that's when the success and money start to flow.

This is an individual process, which is why there's no one surefire path to success in your business. If you've ever created a certain offer because it seemed like a good idea, or started a business based on a plan someone else had massive success with, or copied messaging or strategies because they look pretty damn successful, then I really want you to pay attention to this next part.

You see the amazing achievements of someone else and think that they've finally found the secret 'blueprint' to success and wild levels of income. Then you implement their approach … and wonder why you get different results (read: nowhere near the same financial windfall). It's because that approach and business model worked for *them*. It lit *them* up. It suited *their* strategy needs and goals.

But what worked for them may not work for you, especially if you don't feel energetically aligned and your goal is simply to make money, it will feel hard to sell and hard to attract all that overflowing income. Instead, you need to work out your unique path forward.

Bottom line? Stop chasing the money and connect back to why you started your business in the first place. And remember that chasing success by following the blueprint of someone else's success isn't the way forward. You'll be chasing it for a long time.

Here's the deal. I'm here to change your world and help you believe that ANYTHING is possible. But life is meant to be lived. We're not here solely to fill a bank account. Luckily, I'm over here teaching powerful women how to do BOTH – without burning out or sacrificing life.

Making money for money's sake is not the goal. But let me be clear: big money gets to be a result of the big, bold actions you take to make an impact in this world.

How to Attract More Money

Okay, we've got that out of the way – we now know that making money is not the main goal. Instead, we know that making money is the byproduct of creating a business that has you deeply living in your purpose, where you're so connected and aligned to your ability to make an impact that you create countless opportunities to invite money in.

But how do you start to see those dollars flow into your bank account? Here's the thing: from a young age, most of us are taught not to talk about money. I want to change that narrative, because the more we talk about it, the more we can normalise *huge* levels of wealth as a collective. When I was younger, I would outrightly ask people about money or how much things cost (absolutely no filter – I was curious) only to be met with shock that I had the audacity to ask such a question. It confused me. I was taught at a young age that talking about money or asking someone about money was bad.

Who decided that talking about money was taboo? We celebrate 'authenticity' online when sharing our challenges or failures – yet when people share their money wins or income, it makes them 'superficial', or 'arrogant', or they're 'bragging'. Says who? Usually, these kinds of opinions and reactions are a reflection of what is happening internally for the other person – a reflection of their belief that what has been achieved is NOT possible for them.

Remember, your subconscious mind is powerful – if you tell it you don't need any more money, then that's exactly what you will get. Even though you consciously and actively do want more, if we only think in terms of 'having enough', then that is what we will have and attract. And we know that what we BELIEVE creates our REALITY. So, it's time to change that narrative.

Be honest with yourself about what you really, truly want and dip your toe into Fantasy Land while you imagine just where this new level of wealth could take you. Here are a few ways to lean into your money goals:

- Be grateful for what you have and anchor it with the vision that what you've achieved so far is proof of what you can create in the future.
- Recognise that accumulating more wealth provides greater freedom, reducing stress and enabling you to make a positive impact in the world.
- Take your vision to the next level and imagine what's truly possible. You could make more money and upgrade your lifestyle, share with loved ones and make a bigger impact in the community. The possibilities are endless.

Next, with a clear vision of what you could create and how your life could change with limitless wealth, how do you bridge the gap from *here* to *there* to:

- Create true next level wealth (not just money).
- Fully unblock any underlying money beliefs that are keeping you stuck.
- Feel empowered and in control of your wealth journey, knowing exactly what steps to take to reach your next income level and wealth goal and create abundance.

You first need to build an improved relationship with money.

Once again, this all comes down to shifting your inner world first to see the results in your external world. If you have a belief that wealthy people are somehow separate from you, then you're subconsciously and actively going to sabotage yourself without realising (for all the reasons I outlined in Chapter 4).

Money is like a relationship. Imagine if you're always hiding your partner away from friends and family, leaving them at home when you go out, talking them down or giving them no attention, they probably wouldn't stick around too long, right? That's why it takes shifting our inner beliefs (our inner world becomes our outer) and some simple planning and strategies to attract and retain money.

In the past, I was afraid to talk about money 'too much' because of fear of judgment or fear of triggering the money beliefs of others. I have however realised the more we talk about money, the more we lift up the whole community.

Every time we share our wins and reality, it inspires others to see what can be possible for them.

The louder and prouder we can be, the more we set examples for others and inspire each other to stop playing small. You need to stop repelling money and start inviting it in, you need to change your energy around it and show love to money and wealth. This could mean:

- Respecting money, by knowing how much is coming in and going out.
- Feeling appreciation for it.
- Creating safety around it.
- Enjoying what money brings, rather than feeling any shame or guilt.
- Showing money love. Yep, that's not a typo – you need to give it some TLC.

The more love you show your money, the more it will love you right back. It's a two-way relationship.

Money mantras to build an improved relationship with wealth

I deserve to be paid well for the work I do, and it doesn't have to feel hard.

Money flows to me easily and it feels fun.

Money is infinite in this world, and I am claiming my piece.

My dream clients love paying me well for my expertise.

I deserve to be paid abundantly for what I do, and my clients love to pay me.

Feeling Wealthy Starts NOW

I've explained how you can invite more money in, but there's a crucial part of this process that starts right here, right now. When I see this 'click' with entrepreneurs, I'm reminded that this is truly one of the most impactful mindset lessons you can learn.

You get to feel wildly successful and crazy wealthy where you are *right now*. You get to feel wealthy with the blessings and benefits in your life at this very moment, regardless of the number in your bank account. When you shift your mindset to feeling wealthy exactly where you are now, with what you have today, you'll create an energy around money that invites even more of in. You'll start to experience the joy, healing and abundance that comes with having more – and that then opens the door to receiving even more.

When you have ten times (or 100 times) the income you have right now, you're not going to magically 'feel' happier. Your problems won't magically disappear. You won't suddenly be less busy and things won't magically fall into place. I hate to break it to you, but the phrase 'more money, more problems' is often true. You have bigger stakes at play, more pressure, more staff, more to lose, and more responsibility.

Most people think the process goes something like this: make more money, then solve your problems and be happier. But the secret that truly successful people know is this: you can solve your problems and be happier today, and that creates the energy environment that invites unbelievable levels of wealth, opportunity and prosperity.

What I'm talking about is a complete energetic shift around money; how you invite it and receive it into your life and your business. Your energy around money is such a huge piece of the puzzle when it comes to building and attracting more wealth. And what I want you to know is that you don't have to wait for a certain 'money number' to have fun and freedom in your life. You can choose to feel wealthy right now, today, with exactly what you have – and you can use this gratitude and expansive energy to create even more.

On board with the concept, but unsure how to put it into practice? I'll share some concrete examples. Let's say you dream of being wealthy so you can take your family on 5-star vacations, flying up the pointy end of the plane and living it up in celebrity-filled overseas destinations with limitless cocktails at a beachside resort.

You can have this NOW and start manifesting the deeper benefits you're striving towards. It may not be a $100,000 trip to the other side of the world just yet, but you could plan a vacation to a beachside resort town in Australia, flying business class using the loyalty points you've been saving up, staying in a bougie resort you scored on sale.

It may not look *exactly* like your vision; you're not rubbing shoulders with the Kardashians just yet, and you haven't left the country. But you are starting to enjoy what being wealthy feels like and you're stepping into the expansive feeling of what your life could become. In other words, you're starting to feel wealthy *now*. On the flip side, here's what can happen with the more 'traditional' approach of waiting until *after* the money comes to feel like you've made it. This is Sam's story:

> Sam was one of my coaching clients who was working in her day job while running her digital marketing business on the side. She was earning $2000 per month in her business, racking up the extra hours, and taking on her goals. Within three short months of coaching, she tripled her income and was able to quit her job (without adding more time to her schedule), but everything still felt the same when it came to her feelings about wealth.
>
> In fact, everything felt a bit harder. Earning more money made Sam feel 'heavier': there was more responsibility, more expenses, and more pressure to 'keep it up'. This goes to prove the point, when we are in the mindset of 'there is never enough money' and scarcity is thriving, the number on the outside doesn't change how we feel.
>
> Sam's monthly income went from $2000 to $6000, an amount she would have been over the moon about months earlier. But earning that actual number didn't change how she felt about success or wealth. Without recognising and acting on her ingrained thoughts, beliefs and subconscious triggers, self-sabotage crept in. This is why business owners can experience periods of major growth only to be back where they started

the next month. It's all about recalibrating in line with our Fantasy Land goals and feeling wealthy now.

Yet Sam continued to scale her business to new heights. We shifted her out of her scarcity mindset and set real numbers to the level of income she truly wanted and needed to create the lifestyle she desired; she appreciated the wealth she had created so far. Often people want to skip over this work and get straight to the numbers and strategies, but without the foundations it can be a turbulent ride.

In my own business, I had my first $78,000 cash week in 2022. When it happened, I celebrated (you can count on that). But I didn't necessarily feel any different. I didn't instantly change my buying habits or upgrade my lifestyle – because I had already been living in this expansive energy long before those zeroes hit my bank account.

Some people have absolutely nothing to their name like houses or assets or cash in the bank, but they have joy and abundance in their lives. And there are plenty of rich AF people who certainly don't act or feel successful. We've all heard the quote 'money doesn't buy happiness' and it's 100% true. Money buys things. It buys experiences. It buys upgrades. But money isn't wealth – and to feel genuinely wealthy starts on the inside.

How to feel wealthy NOW

- Ground yourself with the deep belief that you are already wealthy, you are worthy and capable of claiming huge levels of success.

- Know that by focusing on what we want more of, we create more.

- Our subconscious is stubborn and doesn't like to be corrected – as a result, it will funnel all the information that supports its point of view and filter anything else that contradicts it – including opportunities to create more wealth.

- So: we need to work on this now, to avoid the belief that no matter how much cash we have in the bank, it will never be enough.

- To get started, begin to build the proof that you are a wealthy and successful person. Then let the flow-on results from here speak for themselves.

How to step into your wealthy era

Ask yourself:

What makes me feel wealthy?

Where is the evidence, that I am already wealthy?

How can I bring that wealthy energy to my everyday life?

It could be as simple or as complicated as you like, for example:

- Use your fancy glassware.
- Having a bath in the middle of the day.
- Booking a reservation at a fancy restaurant.
- Buying something you always wanted, but never allowed yourself. Hint: even window shopping can help you embody the feeling of wealth.

This helps you anchor into that feeling of wealth NOW.

Then: Expand even further with your Magic Wealth Plan for the future

Jump into Fantasy Land by writing down your Magic Wealth Plan - a complete list (it can be as long or as short as you like) of your big, illogical money goals:

- Maybe it's to bring in ten million in revenue in your business?
- To buy a five million-dollar holiday home on the beach?
- To go on holiday first class for three months and not worry about money.

Whatever you desire, set the intention that you can create it. After you write down your money goals, place them somewhere you can read them and visualise them every day. This helps keep them 'front and centre' in your daily life.

Busting the 'More Money' Myth

Many business owners create 'rules' around what they think they're 'allowed to do' when it comes to money. If this rule is limiting, they can become stuck, and trapped, by the very rule they created which can lead to resentment or burnout instead of chasing down those Fantasy Level goals.

A common limiting rule we've discussed before is: 'If I increase my prices, I will lose all my clients.' It's a myth that selling at a higher price is harder than selling at a lower price point. How do I know this? Working with my clients and based on my personal experience, it's been easier to sign a dream client at $50,000 than it was to sell misaligned clients at $100.

When I first started coaching, I charged $100. That's not a typo, it was $100. And I found it so hard to sell because I wasn't fully grounded in it. Now, I have people entering my world and happily paying over $50,000 – and that price will continue to increase, because I'm always growing and evolving, chasing my Fantasy Land goals. This change came about through a combination of inner work, understanding my value, overcoming self-sabotage and communicating my worth through authority-based marketing.

Sometimes, it can feel like you're already more expensive than your competitors or that there's no potential to change your pricing because you're at the higher end of the scale, or maybe you have had a recent price increase. But you need to remember, it's your business and you make the moves that serve you, which will ultimately serve your clients too. This is Lisa's story:

Lisa, an energy healer, was ready to give up a whole income stream in her business. She didn't enjoy offering this service in her business anymore; it took up way too much time and she wanted to put her energy into her other service offering. It would have been super easy for me to say 'Okay, stop offering that', but I knew there was a deeper reason she felt this way.

I asked her: 'If you were paid ten times the price that you are currently earning from this service, would you enjoy it? Or if money was not a factor, would you enjoy this work? Did she believe that her expertise was worth a higher price point?' Lisa's response was yes to all my questions. She also believed that her product offering was definitely worth more. But on a deeper level, resentment was beginning to build because she had created a 'rule' where she believed it was impossible to charge more for that service. Why? Because no one else in her industry was.

As soon as Lisa understood the disparity between her 'rule' and her true desire to earn more for that service, we were able to shift her pricing and value proposition to ensure she was paid a reasonable amount. And guess what? Clients continued to sign up with no questions asked. Her rule wasn't 'real' at all.

It all boils down to this: when you know you're the BEST at what you do, and you know there is limitless money to be made and wealth to be created, then you know there is no cap to the amount you can charge. So channel that high ticket leader energy and own it like Beyonce.

Practical Tools and Tips to Make More Money

I want you to know that illogical levels of wealth are already available to you, and it's your time to claim it.

So how do you go about this at a practical level? The way I coach is always a combination of the inner mindset work and practical strategies; I don't believe it's one or the other. We've already taken a deep dive into the mindset work, so now, I want to share some practical tools and processes you can use to boost your wealth.

Whatever your goal is, do you have a plan and know exactly how you will get there? Or are you trying to grow your business without any real plan or clear path as to how? I often see people who want to grow their business, but they don't know how. So instead they end up hustling and working extra hard and if they hit the goal at the end of the year, fantastic! And if those goals aren't achieved then they try harder the next year. And the hustle continues. Most of the time they are leaving their success to chance. The problem with this is that there is a high possibility you may not reach your goals – or if you do, you'll be burnt out and completely exhausted.

Being suffocated by the everyday grind is not going to unleash your big Fantasy Goals, quite the reverse.

One of my coaching clients was working harder than ever, and making great money, but she had no room for growth and no energy left. She felt stuck inside her own business, with nowhere to go and no idea what to do next. This is a common problem for entrepreneurs, especially women in business, and it's one of the elements I love about coaching: from the outside, I could see exactly what steps were needed to restructure her business, pricing and income, to not only grow her revenue but also to reclaim her time and freedom.

This type of game-changing life unlock is possible for you, too.

The key lies in stepping into making energetic shifts to transform your mindset, review what you already have and then taking a huge leap and going all in!

Turn Plans into Action

The biggest mistake that we can make in achieving our goals is having no set plan around profit planning, pricing, or income. Guess what? You can reverse engineer it. I am going to show you how to build out your business and reach your income goals, without leaving it to chance – and without working more time and hustling harder!

This is something I work deeply on with my clients; my superpower is to help people discover the core of what they want so we can create a personalised roadmap to make it happen. Every person is different when it comes to their goals, their desires and the impact they make with their business, so there's no 'one size fits all' solution.

But there are strategies and techniques you can use which pack the pages of this book. And what I really want you to know – what I want you to truly, deeply feel in your bones – is that anything is possible when you are clear on where you are going and build your business model around your Fantasy Land goals. Grab your journal and let's get planning to take action.

——— ♀ ———

Your Wealth goals

Step 1: Review your current situation and income structure.

- Work out how many sales or clients you need to hit your goals based on your current prices. How many hours will that require from you? Is it sustainable?

- Doing this exercise will provide perspective and assist you in making the necessary changes. It could be that your business model or pricing cannot sustain the growth and may need to restructure to allow the freedom you desire.

- It may require a massive shift, or some small tweaks, or often when I do this activity with my clients, they realise their goals are way too small and are much easier to attain than they once thought.

Step 2: Set your goal income/revenue for the year.

- Set BIG goals – remember, we don't play small.
- Detach from the outcome – this is very different to giving up and not trying.

Step 3: Break it down into monthly income goals.

- This should grow month by month; don't just divide step 2 by 12!
- Keep in mind promotions or seasonality of your business, some months will be larger than others.

Step 4: Get even more specific on HOW.

- Break it down into products or services that you need to sell.
- This makes it a lot more achievable. And gives you a step-by-step guide to reach.
- By doing this, you can easily identify where to focus your marketing activities to increase control over hitting your goals, rather than waiting until the end of the month and leaving it to chance.

Step 5: Review

- Check your numbers – is it achievable? If not, return to step 1.
- Do you need a TONNE of customers to hit your financial goal?
- If you cannot supply or service that many customers, you need to increase your prices or shift your business model.
- If your goals are very easy to achieve, then dream way bigger.

As you go through this process, remember to always choose to operate from a place of abundance and opportunity, not scarcity and fear.

———————

Key Insights

- There can be taboo energy around the topic of money, and a lot of conditioning and limiting beliefs we need to unpack to set ourselves up for true financial success.

- Making money for money's sake is not the goal. Big money is a result of the big, bold actions you take to make an impact in this world.

- Feeling wealthy comes first, then the money flows. Having ten times (or 100 times) the income you have right now will not magically make you 'feel' more wealthy or happier. Your problems won't magically disappear. You won't suddenly be less busy.

- You may be subconsciously repelling money – but there are steps you can take to turn this around and invite more money into your life, starting now.

I don't subscribe to the idea of failure –
because I don't allow myself to create stories
about what that means about me.

True leadership is showing up, *especially* *when* **things get hard.**

CHAPTER 7

Keep Going

I'm going to give it to you straight: the future is completely in your hands.

The actions you're taking today will determine your future outcomes. That means it's crucial to stay committed, even when you haven't seen the results yet. When it comes to the 'keep going' part of running a business, where it feels hard and you're still building towards the results you want – I can relate. I've been there – many times – welcome to entrepreneurship. But I've been able to keep creating more success in my business because I am always looking forward; I'm always making big moves; I'm always excited about what might come next, even when the outcomes of my previous actions are still unclear.

The biggest mistake I see for business owners that can interfere with our unstoppable success is trying to play it safe. When you don't see instant results in your business, or your goals, you might feel compelled to step back into playing small because it feels safer. I'm sure you know what I'm talking about: maybe you've launched a new product or service, and you didn't get the immediate response you were hoping for, so you decided to stop promoting it. Or you're chasing a certain higher-level client, but your enquiries are coming from those who don't have the budget to work with you and as a reflex, you revert to your previous lower prices. I see you, and I know it's a frustrating cycle.

When you can't see the results yet, it can feel downright uncomfortable. Your ego begins to freak out, and that's when self-sabotage comes in. But you don't have to let it win.

If you want to play big, you need to be committed to the vision – on the good days and especially the bad days.

When things are uncomfortable, you have two choices. The first one is easier. It's the well-trodden path: a retreat to comfort. You're uncomfortable, so it makes sense to return to where the comfort is, right? Or there's another choice. A harder choice. But one that is more fulfilling, more satisfying, more aligned with your values and goals and ultimately, one that leads you to far more success and builds major resilience. That choice is to lean in deeper and grow.

How do you do this? You hold the trust. You feel the discomfort. And you show up anyway. I guarantee that it will feel like magic when the results start flowing in. But let me tell you a secret – it's not magic. It's the fact that you stay committed when everyone else gives up. This sounds amazing in theory, but what you really need are the tools, tips and techniques to help navigate those hard days and to build on the momentum and success you're creating to achieve even bigger goals. Strap yourself in because this chapter is going to deliver everything you need to know.

Congruence – Your Secret Weapon

Often, you know exactly what you need to hit your goals. I'm sure that if I asked you right now what you have been procrastinating about – something you know you *should* be doing, but for some reason it never gets done – there might be one action (or more) that instantly comes to mind, right?

When you're putting off the big Fantasy Goals that could change your business, in a good way, you're being incongruent. Incongruency is when you say you want something or set a certain goal yet aren't living up to it. On the flip side, congruence is when you say you value or want something and you live according to that intention through your actions.

Some of the ways incongruency can 'show up' are:

- Saying you want to have more money but refusing to increase your pricing.
- Saying you want financial freedom but spending money on Gucci handbags when you don't have enough to pay your massive tax bill.
- Lacking energy and wanting to be healthier but believing that eating healthy is hard and expensive.
- Wanting more free time and relaxation, but you can't delegate because you think you're the only person who can ensure that everything is perfect.
- Saying you want massive growth and Fantasy Land results but procrastinating on your current goals and projects by spending time on 'busy work'.

Does anything here resonate for you? Noticing this in ourselves is crucial to our success, but sometimes it can be hard to recognise.

If we cannot fully see where we are incongruent, it makes it very difficult to realign and take action toward becoming limitless.

It can be easy to identify incongruency in others – maybe someone comes to mind right now, someone who you know says they want to achieve substantial goals, maybe even Fantasy Land level goals, and yet you watch them do nothing about it. It's so frustrating to watch others say one thing and do another. Yet, we could be (read: definitely are) doing the same thing to ourselves and turning a blind eye.

Why is it, though, that congruence can be such a tricky thing for us to fully embrace? Often, it comes back to the fact that we don't want to believe we are flaky or that we're not taking as much bold action as we think we are (say hello to your ego trying to preserve its current perception of self).

If you want to create truly limitless success, you need to be congruent.

When you are congruent, amazing things happen.

This is because:

- You have the deepest self-trust, so when you set an intention, you know you'll make it happen and follow it through.

- Your confidence goes through the roof.

- Your energy and desire to make a difference increase dramatically.

- You feel at peace that you are going about life with intention.

- Decisions become easy to make.

- Your goals start to fall into place.

Here's what happens when you're *incongruent*. First, your brain knows that you're procrastinating. Your brain is like your supervisor; she's watching everything you're doing and noting it down in her little notepad. Every time you commit to something but then don't do what you say or don't pursue the goals that you want to or value, she's taking note and logging it away into her trusty 'perception of self' journal.

For instance, if you feel like you're a go-getter and an action taker, yet you procrastinate on making a decision for two weeks, your subconscious mind takes note. She uses this incongruence to create a proof of reasons to not be confident. I mean, think about it: if your subconscious sees you as someone who can't keep their word, is not confident and changes their mind every time someone questions them: Well, this is going to impact the way you show up, right?

Congruence goes hand in hand with consistency, and if you're not showing up consistently, your results will be limited. This can become a vicious cycle because, after your subconscious notes your incongruence, it creates a lack of self-trust within yourself, which will impact your results.

When I shared this concept in one of my sessions, it clicked for a number of my clients, and they launched into bold action around business goals they had been putting off for months – or even years. One client took instant action and presented her client with her new increased rates and secured a $10,000 deal within 24 hours. Another client launched an offer she had been sitting on for months, and another one immediately increased her prices, which tripled her income.

This is why I'm so passionate about this work and this concept of congruence: I want to share some of this fire energy with you

to catapult you into big, bold, meaningful action toward your
Fantasy Land goals.

Where can you be more congruent?

Are you reading along and realising that you are being
incongruent right now?

Here are a few questions to ask yourself to stir this pot
and give your supervisor (aka your brain) evidence of
a whole new perception of self:

- Where have I been incongruent?
- What are examples of me saying I'll do something
  and yet I don't do it?
- What things am I frustrated about right now, yet am
  not doing much to change it?
- What goals or desires have you been struggling to
  achieve?

Journal your answers. Now go out there and take some
big bold action toward congruency and see how much
shifts for you.

What to Do When Emotions Take Over

Our emotional state impacts our ability to act; it's easy to take
bold steps and make bold decisions when we feel good, when
things are going well and when success flows easily.

But it's much harder to do this when we are emotionally
unstable. These are the times when we're more likely to be
questioning everything we do. It's also straight-up harder to dig
into your stories of self-belief and show up when people criticise
you, make a complaint, or want a refund. That's the tough thing
about being in business. It's easy to show up when everyone is

buying and it's easy to believe in yourself when your loved ones are supportive. But this is real life, and it's not always smooth sailing. Sometimes, we can make the mistake of forgetting that when it comes to the hard parts of running a business – you're not alone!

I have had numerous occasions where it felt as though customers weren't buying as quickly as I'd like them to.

I have received criticism and hateful messages, more than once – and as much as I know it's not about me and it's all about them, it still hurts, right? When things aren't going the way we want them to, we feel it in our nervous system. We feel on edge and sometimes, when our emotions enter the conversation, it can change the way we feel like showing up.

The key is showing up anyway.

It's NOT about you. You need to be resilient when things make you doubt yourself: when sales feel stagnant, when you feel like an imposter or when you're dealing with challenges like debt, disappointment or different outcomes than you expected.

Imagine feeling so grounded in who you are and where you're going, that these challenges are just a blip on your radar, and they don't send you into a self-doubt spiral every time they happen.

This is the level of resilience and being grounded we get to build, because no matter what stage of business you are at, there are major challenges the whole way – it's just about how you handle them. The bigger and more successful your business gets, the higher the stakes. There's no way to avoid challenges, setbacks or missteps. But you can adjust the way you respond to them.

To weather these storms, you need to build your resilience so you're able to show up, even when you don't get validation:

- When clients don't tell you how amazing you are every week.
- When clients don't react to your offers and buy up a storm.
- When there is limited interaction with your social media posts.
- When you receive criticism.
- When people think your prices are too high – or even say you are ripping people off.

There's no denying these situations can hurt. But quite often, it's not the actual situation that has us swimming in our emotions, it's the stories we create about it.

For instance, when people aren't buying, you could make it mean:

- I'm a bad business owner.
- I'm not capable of making sales.
- People don't trust me enough to want to learn from me or buy from me.
- People must find me annoying, so I should stop selling.

Or if someone tells you your price is too high, you begin to think:

- I shouldn't be charging this much.
- They're right – I'm not even worth it.
- I have no right to charge these prices.
- There are so many people doing this who are a better investment than me.

Don't create these stories in your mind when they don't exist. It's up to YOU to decide what is going on – you're in the driver's seat and you have the power to choose your next step. I want to share an experience that happened in my first business when I was pitching for wholesale deals directly with buyers. I compiled a list of over 1000 emails and then I began emailing, one at a time, with all the excitement in the world about the opportunities these potential contacts held.

I personalised every one of those emails and religiously followed up with each of them at least four or five times over a period of six months (persistence is key – I didn't just give up after emailing three companies in one day, this was not an example of instant gratification culture but tenacity). After a grand total of 5000 emails were sent and waiting a whole year, I received one reply, and they said 'no'. At that point, I could've told myself – what's the point? No one is interested. But instead, I looked at the facts (no one replied to my email), I stripped away any emotional reaction and continued to email more people. We could make assumptions all day around why people haven't replied, or we can continue to follow up and email more to get to that 'yes'.

All the evidence was there that my strategy wasn't working, but I was determined. After 12 months of perseverance, even when I saw no proof or results, I finally received one email back from a major retailer saying: 'Yes, we'll give you a go'. They wanted a trial order of – wait for it – USD$30,000 – this was huge in my first year of business.

Persistence, big Fantasy Land thinking, and an unshakeable belief all played a part in landing my first major deal with a key retailer. That one deal opened doors for me and for this reason, I don't consider a single email that I sent or a single moment that I spent chasing up non-starters to be wasted.

Now I don't recommend pushing forward for 12 months with a strategy that is not working, but in this specific example, at that time, the only way open to me was to secure wholesale deals by directly contacting buyers – so that's what I did. Plus, I was also working in tandem on building my brand awareness and trust in the background to land these deals. The takeaway message here isn't to keep going at all costs but is a story of persistence and showing up *even when* the results are not evident yet.

I don't subscribe to the idea of failure – because I don't allow myself to create stories about what that means about me. But how about you? Are you going to let your made-up stories stop you from making your big, dreamy goals happen? Or are you going to put them aside and take that bold action?

It takes a whole lot of energy to sit and play the victim when you could use that energy to change your situation.

That starts with having confidence and resilience. Pure confidence and leadership happen when we know who we are and *nothing else* shakes us. You decide the narrative.

Take back your power

Ask yourself:

What do you make it mean when you are feeling low?

Do you change the game plan when things aren't going as well as you would like?

Do you hide away when someone doubts you, or stop selling because no one has purchased yet?

Reflect on the questions and write your answers in your journal.

There is often an unconscious part of our mind that makes an event, a conversation, or a situation into a story about us. It's dangerous and unhelpful to let your external world change how you see yourself and how you show up. When times are tough, remind yourself: what was the game plan and what were you going to do when you were fresh and motivated? The circumstances may have changed but DO IT ANYWAY.

Remember: you don't have to wait until everything feels amazing – most of us do this backwards.

It's easy to fall into the trap that to feel good we first need that money, that new client, new house, new relationship, new car, whatever it is we want – quite often things feel better when we just do the damn thing first.

True leadership is:

- Showing up, even when things get hard.
- Not taking everything personally.
- Feeling powerful and confident, even when your situation isn't rosy.
- Taking action based on the facts, not your emotions.

Levelling up Into Your Limitless Self

When you start to grow, make big moves and step more into your limitless self, the voice of fear will create new edges and challenges for you to continue to transcend and grow.

Have you ever felt like you're ready for a whole new level of success; then it seems like the hardest thing to do and challenges are showing up all over the place?

It's not always an easy path and resistance to moving forward with your goals and growth shows up in different, sometimes very sneaky ways. For instance, in my own business, it seems like every time I plan to start charging more and increase my prices, I have had a bunch of people tell me it's too expensive. I could've very easily stepped back into safety and kept my prices down, but I chose to level up. Whenever I decide to launch a new program, step into my authority, and own my expertise in a certain area, I experience major challenges in *that* exact area.

The first time I launched my Limitless Mindset program, which was all about building inner resilience and unlocking the deeper mindset blocks that allow us to reach major levels of success, I had a very nasty online post directed right, at, me. In the very same week that I was launching my major program, I was faced with this very negative review – this REALLY challenged my mindset.

I had a multitude of friends send me the post, as it was very obviously about me. The comments flowed in, with other people jumping onto the bandwagon. In the past, that post would have sent me into a major self-doubt spiral and had me hide away for weeks. Fortunately, I've worked hard on these fears, so at that moment, I didn't feel too phased by it. Did it sit in the back of my mind? Sure. Was I losing sleep over it? Not a wink.

Initially, I certainly experienced thoughts that I should just hide away, not post on social media or promote my soon-to-be-launched program, but I very quickly transcended those thoughts and showed up exactly as I'd intended. In these moments it's not about being some sort of robot with no emotions, it's about building our strength and resilience to hold these challenges and move through them. Rather than it taking me weeks to move past, I had moved it to the back of my mind within a few hours ... that being said, it doesn't mean these things don't hurt a little.

It is incredibly important to remember that you are NOT alone. Many business owners have experienced negative feedback, it could be whenever they step into the next level, such as increase their prices, start to claim their expertise or be bolder. Challenges have tested them every single time, but with intentional mindset work it is possible to transcend the blocks, come out the other side and be so much better off for it.

Whenever we go through periods of levelling up, we can be prepared for the challenges that may come along with it. In this type of situation, you have two options:

1. Stay stuck there and let your situation or circumstances (and other people's point of view) define you.

2. Transcend up and choose to see the challenges as an opportunity to step even more into your next level limitless self.

For example, with increasing your prices and having people tell you it's too expensive:

If you choose option 2, then you may lose some clients and have less income in the short term – that's a potential reality. Now, you have a choice, you can see this as a problem and hold tighter onto the clients you do have, come at everything with a scarcity or limited mindset, infuse this scarcity energy into the vibes you are putting out, and start to assume it'll be hard to get more new clients.

OR

You see this as an opportunity to step up into your highest self – where you get excited by the challenge to build your resilience and self-trust, as you make big moves that are congruent with your next-level self. When you are the badass charging much higher prices, chances are there will be more people who can't afford your prices. By holding your self-trust in those moments, it shows your subconscious that you can handle the challenges that come with your next level.

It's the same problem with two very different mindsets. We know what we think and believe becomes our reality, so we know that each line of thinking will also result in two very different outcomes.

Think of it this way: it's building your strength to hold that next level of success. Imagine if you went to the gym with a goal of lifting 100kg, but every time you went, you chose the 5kg weights. You turned up every day so you were consistent, but you were also always lifting the exact same weight wondering why you're still not able to achieve the goal to lift 100kg.

If we never face the challenges head on, we will never be able to hold and be grounded in our next level.

If you want to reach that 100kg goal, you need to step up the weight each time, get out of your comfort zone and hold a little more than you know you can. Ultimately, this builds the strength you need.

How to Be Your Most Magnetic Self

Magnetism is one of your secret weapons as a business owner. It's highly undervalued and often overlooked, but magnetism is a powerful way to stay connected to your clients, your purpose, and your goals.

Think about it: when we focus on creating fun and joy, people are magnetised to us. But sometimes, business can feel super heavy. In these moments, instead of focusing on fun and the impact we have, we concentrate on achieving set goals no matter what. This is when 'keeping going' in business can start to feel like a real slog.

In these moments, we stop ourselves from having fun or experiencing happiness and instead, push harder until we check that goal off our list. That energy we're carrying – the work harder, hustle more, win at all costs energy – can flow through to the way we show up for people. Often, it works and by pushing hard for results, we reach our goal. Then, we quickly move on to the next goal and repeat this pattern all over again!

It's not a fun way to create success. And the irony is that when we work like this, we have it backwards. We can try so hard to be magnetic, to grow our business and create big success, that we can lose sight of what makes us magnetic (which is ultimately what draws people to work with us).

Picture this: You have two friends, and they couldn't be more different. One is always a bit of a downer. She just feels heavy to be around and is always super serious and critical of you. The other friend shines with warm, fun energy and makes you feel your best – you always feel uplifted after interacting with them. Which person feels more magnetic? Which person would you rather spend time with and buy from? Both friends are parts of you.

We all go through periods when we are lit up and excited by what we are doing, and that energy pours out of us. It's infectious and uplifting to be around. And we also go through times when we feel like burning everything to the ground. In these moments, we can get so caught up in being super serious, finding new strategies, and just pushing harder to achieve the goals we've set that we lose sight of what we're trying to accomplish in the first place. Hint: it's not stress, pressure, and a laser focus on winning at all costs.

I often advise my clients in times when they feel heavy and there appears to be no momentum in their business to stop pushing. And return to being the most magnetic *YOU*. Make it your priority to create fun energy, even when things aren't working out the way you planned or when sales haven't arrived yet.

Remove the pressure for everything to work out exactly as you planned – it never will, so you might as well have fun with it and strap in for the ride!

Sometimes, you need to step away from your everyday life to gain this perspective. This is Jenn's story:

> Jenn once came to me feeling burnt out, deflated and lacking motivation in her growing e-commerce product-based business. She was juggling kids, a full-time job and a thriving business and she had (unsurprisingly) hit her limit. In other words: she was feeling anything but magnetic.
>
> She came onto the call with me, ready for me to kick her up the butt, to light a fire and tell her to just keep pushing and she was shocked when I said the complete opposite. She was pouring from an empty cup and the way I see it, it's impossible to show up as the most vibrant, connected

and lit-up version of yourself and your clients if you're not living in that magnetised energy day-to-day.

As you know by now, there is always a deeper reason for *why* we lack motivation and when we get these alarm bells ringing from our mind and body, it's a sign that something is misaligned. Jenn wasn't having any fun or taking care of herself, and she felt disconnected from her business.

My advice to Jenn was to take a two-day solo retreat; note this was a very personalised suggestion to her because I know the way her brain works and how she best recuperates. Disappearing off the grid for a couple of days may be your vibe too, or it might not align, the point is to recognise the moments you need to switch up or need to nurture yourself, and then making the time to re-fill your cup.

Jenn booked a hotel away from her daily life and near her happy place: the beach. At first, I told her to do *nothing*: no work, no thinking about her to-do list, just a complete break from reality to reset her nervous system and allow her mind space to regain clarity. On the second day, after she'd recalibrated, I set her tasks to reconnect with her business. She came out of that experience re-set, fully refreshed and having absolute clarity on the way forward.

Now, if I had told Jenn to keep pushing and hustling, to outsource, get some more support and keep striving towards her goals – which, honestly is not uncommon in the coaching space – she would have continued to deplete her energy and feel even more out of touch with her life and business. That, to me, is a recipe for disaster.

This is my gentle reminder to you to check in with yourself and notice what you need right now to feel your best. You may not need to invest in a weekend away to reconnect like Jenn, but even a morning at the beach, a few hours in nature or an afternoon blocked out to focus could help give you the clarity you need. You may discover that you're sacrificing things you truly need in your life such as love, connection, fun or health. These are usually the things that find their way to the bottom of the pile the fastest.

All of that said, I need to be crystal clear: there is a BIG difference between taking the time out to regain your magnetism and focus versus procrastinating because your fear is speaking loudly. It's up to you to work out when you need to feel the fear and do the damn thing anyway, and when to go and have some fun.

One other quick reminder: you do not have to be anyone else to be magnetic.

Being magnetic is about becoming the highest version of you; someone that your dream clients *need* to work with. Before anyone else can see your magic, you need to see it first. If you are unsure or not confident in what you are offering others can feel that uncertainty. Energy doesn't lie. For example:

- When sales or kicking goals in your business feels fun, and easy and doesn't result in burnout, we feel absolutely on fire.
- This energy enables momentum to build, and we become confident to do all sorts of things – like to ask for more, to negotiate better terms or more money, or to lean into selling and marketing in a bigger way.

- This momentum builds because the energy you're creating around your goals is expansive.
- The key to building momentum lies in being consistent and not forcing outcomes. Have fun and show up authentically and your ideas, content and messages will be overflowing.

How to build momentum, even when you think there's none.

Look at what you are currently doing, who you are, what you love, and why you are good at what you do. Over time we can forget this, so it's a great exercise for overall mindset as well as being able to step back into the energy of why people need what you are selling.

Then consider how can you become *more* obsessed with your brand and offer and sell confidently. Get your journal and make an extensive list. Some thought-starters to help you:

- Remember why you started.
- Consider why the way that you do it is different and better.
- Focus on why you are amazing at what you do.
- Ponder how you would be showing up if the sales were flowing in with ease (note: this is how you should be showing up every day)
- Thinking about the lives you have transformed (testimonials and messages are great to keep in a file somewhere to reignite your spark)
- Bring more fun to everyday mundane tasks.

When you step into this Big Boss energy, you invite sales to flow in – when you come from this energy, it releases the pressure to sell and is even more magnetic.

What to Do When it All Seems Too Hard

Okay, so you have been giving it everything. You've been selling and promoting your offer or service; days and weeks begin to pass and no one has purchased (or not as many as you'd hoped).

You're all in, so you keep telling yourself to stay positive. You draw on all of your tools, techniques and strategies to drive more sales, and you tell yourself that they will start to come … eventually. But there's still a part of you that feels scared. The part that doubts the next level of sales or opportunities is going to come. Ever. Then a little more time passes, and imposter syndrome creeps in.

You might even stop selling because what is the point, right? No one wants what you have to offer anyway. You see other people kicking goals and making huge strides forward in their business, and resentment begins to set in. It sets itself up for a little pity party and invites self-doubt to come and hang out.

I've helped so many clients walk this path and as you may have gathered, the first step is showing up anyway – even when you don't see immediate results. Having deep trust in yourself and your direction is so crucial, now more than ever. To do this, you need to build confidence by building emotional intelligence. This empowers you to move past the feelings of resentment, comparison or self-doubt. None of that matters because you have radical self-belief.

Remember: to truly believe something is true, your subconscious likes to see proof. So, look for all of the proof and evidence of your success – even if it isn't tangible yet. This could be potential clients saying they want to sign up, but they haven't yet: this is evidence that what you offer has a market and people are interested in buying from you. (PS If this is happening for you – make sure you have a clear strategy and process to follow up and ask for that sale). Or it might be previous clients talking about working with you. Don't fixate on the outcome but take the proof of the impact you made.

You need to focus on the fact that even when people aren't buying, the marketing activities and connections that you are creating are working to build your overall brand. You might not be having short term wins and instant sales, but you are building long-term brand awareness and lasting trust around you being the go-to expert for your business services or products.

Effort Now Creates Future Results

It's all a compound effect. When you have a deep knowledge of what's possible, you realise that even when you don't see the immediate results, your consistent effort, and your commitment to taking action will eventually pay off, as they equal the results you see in the future.

For instance, I once began promoting a new offer on a Monday and I heard absolute crickets (it happens at every stage of business – I promise you, even my multi-seven-figure business friends experience this). By Friday I was at the beach, and I received not one but three enquiries about that offer, one of which included a screenshot of my promotion from my Instagram story on Monday: my future client had saved it in her phone and was thinking about it all week. This is proof that you often won't see immediate results – but that shouldn't change your approach or strategy. I kept showing up and stayed grounded in my offer and I saw three new clients join that Friday.

The results may not always happen immediately, but the idea is the same regardless. Deep self-beliefs translate to the results you get, now and in the future. And YOU get to choose which energy gains momentum. Will it be the subconscious voices that tell you you're not good enough; that keep you stuck in comparison and lack; that have you focusing on what's going wrong? Or will it be the inner knowing that you're on the right track; that you're capable, confident and you have something incredible to offer; that every step forward you take is another step closer towards success?

Create your list of evidence

It can be motivating to gather evidence that your success is coming. Look for concrete proof that success is around the corner: emails you've received, meetings you've booked, clients you've spoken to and prospects who have made contact.

Write it down. When your mind sees things written down, it adds a powerful element of realness: Dr. Gail Matthews, a psychology professor at Dominican University in California, found that you are 42% more likely to achieve your goals just by writing them down.

I know we're technically not talking about goals here, but it's in the same lane. So, get writing!

Key Insights

- Congruence is when you say you value something or want something, and you live according to that intention in your actions. It is your secret weapon!

- Most people think that confidence comes AFTER success, which isn't true. To become confident, you need to take consistent action and invest in doing the inner work.

- When we focus on creating fun and joy, people are magnetised to us. Make it your priority to have fun with what you are doing, even when things aren't working out the way you planned.

- It's harder to have self-belief and show up when people criticise you, make a complaint, or want a refund. These situations can hurt - but often it's the stories we create about them that hurt most.

- To move past the feelings of resentment, comparison or self-doubt, our subconscious likes to see proof. So, look for all of the proof and evidence of your success (even if it isn't tangible yet).

The road to success is not LOGICAL.
And that's why those who are adaptable,
willing to try something new and aren't afraid
to 'fail' will continue to create more success
than those who aren't. Period.

CHAPTER 8

Why I Love 'Failing' (and you will too)

I want to tell you something that might sound crazy ... I don't believe in failure. Seriously, I don't.

I often see people talking about their 'biggest failures', and I've had people ask me in interviews about my failures. I've been asked to write about them or record a podcast focused on failing, but it's something I've always felt resistance to – not because I don't like sharing the challenges – I am a completely open book (and an oversharer in the best way) – but because I cannot think of any failures.

It's just NOT how my brain works. In my mind, failure just doesn't exist – and that's not some cute inspirational quote – it's just how I've always operated. When I sat down to try and make a list of my 'failures', my mind was completely blank.

I get why people want to hear about failures, and why successful people are often quick to share theirs. And, as I previously shared, we celebrate 'authenticity' when that means talking about hardship and struggle because underneath it all there is often a desire to feel less alone in our challenges. But if you're sharing 'failures' purely to make your success more palatable to others (Hello, Tall Poppy), then who is that serving?

> **Have I had challenges, setbacks, lost money, and tough times? You bet. But I've never seen any of these experiences as failures.**

When I'm experiencing a hard or challenging moment in my business, my brain goes into logical fixing mode. All I see is my next step and the way forward. 'Failure' as others might label it, is just another step in the process toward success because when we remove ego (the protector of our concept of self) from the equation and don't create stories about ourselves in the situation, failure simply cannot exist. Instead, it becomes merely a circumstance and an opportunity for growth and learning.

The way your brain stores memories is based on the meaning and emotion that you label and give those stories. It's the most complex library system you've ever seen, and my 'failure' shelf is empty, simply because I've never felt like I've failed.

In those moments where I was asked to share my 'failures', I felt as though I was almost reframing my story just to make it into a 'failure' – when to me, it simply wasn't how I saw it. It felt heavy, and I began to think, if it makes me feel like this for just five seconds, that's too much of my energy wasted, and I do not have time for that! Why would I try and make the challenges seem harder or more traumatic than it was at the time just to get people to sympathise or relate to me?

Failure? Never. It's all Lessons

Remember at the beginning of this book about having zero (less than zero) dollars to my name? Well, even then I didn't once think

I was a failure. Sure, I had a big old cry and called my mum, but then I moved on with the plan as if my goals were inevitable, and guess what? Everything worked out because I acted and believed it would. However, I didn't create a story or belief around what the situation meant about me. Instead, I stuck to the facts.

Fact: I spent all the money in my account in pursuit of my big goals.

Story: I'm not good with money (which isn't true at all).

Laura's Lesson

Laura, an online course creator, came to me feeling so deflated about the state of her business. She had just launched her newest offer, and no one was buying. Enter the storytelling: she started convincing herself there wasn't a consumer for her product, the offer wasn't good enough, she shouldn't bother moving forward with it and her direction in business was lost.

We sat down and broke down the facts. It came down to one simple fact. No one had purchased it. (Yet). That was it! When we stripped the emotion away and looked at the facts, it opened her mind to solving the problems. Laura had two choices: take the stories she was telling herself as truth and give up. Or continue to sell her offer and completely get behind it – shift her messaging, undertake promotions and work toward achieving greater awareness and sales.

After revisiting how all of this sat with her values and goals, Laura stepped up, chose the second option and achieved sales above her expectations. This never would have been her reality if she chose the first option – playing safe and buying into the idea that she had failed would have derailed a business growth success that she simply had to turn up for.

Jenny's Lesson

Jenny, a go-getter in spiritual healing and tarot, came into one of our mentoring sessions with her motivation was at an all-time low. In previous sessions we had mapped out a major collaboration deal for her business, really leaning into her Fantasy Land goals, Jenny was all in. She had taken the plans and had invested so much energy and intention into achieving the goals. For Jenny, sending this collaboration pitch made her step outside her comfort zone. But she had hit the ground running, undertaking in-depth research and creating an extensive and engaging pitch deck.

After a few days passed by and she hadn't heard back, she began feeling nervous. I nudged her to follow up, so she sent off another two emails over the coming weeks. During our mentoring session, she shared that she finally received a reply, which she anxiously opened ... and it was a 'no'.

They didn't believe the proposal was a good fit. This feedback sent her into a spiral of self-doubt and played into her feelings of failure – the stories she had subconsciously taught herself were lying in wait ready to take over. 'All in' Jenny was now scrambling. The story she told herself was that 'her brand wasn't good enough to work with a high-profile brand'. The flow-on effect was that she believed her brand would not be 'good enough' for other major collaboration opportunities. Jenny was knee-deep and sinking fast into self-doubt, sabotage and feelings of failure, doubting that she would ever achieve success.

Our session quickly turned into a recalibration opportunity. Again, we brought it back to the facts: she had emailed one brand – just one – out of millions of possibilities, and they simply said it was not the right fit. This has nothing to do with her brand, being good enough, or being able to work with larger brands than her. When she looked at the facts, it lifted that doubt for her and with mindset work (refer to Chapter 4), she felt empowered to reach out to a bunch more. Within a couple of weeks, she secured an even bigger partnership, one that aligned with her business goals and allowed her to step into her next level of visibility and confidence.

If you have ever had a moment when you begin to doubt if your Fantasy Land goals will ever be possible, just know that you are not alone and there is always a pathway forward. Take a moment to pause, separate the facts from the stories and meanings you have attached, and then make the moves that you know you are capable of. Sometimes things will work out even better than you ever imagined.

Focus on the facts

Next time you face a challenge, or you feel like you've failed, separate the facts from the stories or meanings you've created about it.

Your subconscious will believe what you feed it and take whichever story you choose as the absolute truth. In my example, if I had focused on the story 'I'm not good with money', I would have become closed off to new opportunities that could potentially prove my subconscious wrong (and it doesn't like to be wrong!).

When you focus on the story bound in a limiting belief, you're limiting yourself. But if you focus only on the facts, there are many ways forward – and that's where we want to play.

When Failure Costs a Fortune

One of the biggest fears we have around failure is about losing money. This makes complete sense, of course you don't want to be out of pocket, or make business decisions that don't deliver a strong return on investment.

But loss is all about perspective. When you run a business at a high level, and invest in yourself and your business consistently and make those fast moves (like the empowered badass CEO that you are), there will be times when the moves or investments just don't work out. Without some level of risk, there can't be a reward – it's simply how you GROW.

I can't even remember all the times I have made decisions in my business that have been less than exceptional. But let me tell you, it's NO small amount. Although I've never had zero dollars in my bank account again since that first experience (I've made sure of that), there are plenty of times I've 'lost' money in my business. I've had events cancelled at the last minute and I've lost thousands of dollars on catering and set-up deposits and booking fees.

I've invested in 'Done-For-You' services that turned out to be unsuitable, one size fits all, generic services that didn't work out well at all. I've paid big bucks for fancy photoshoots where the results were so far from what I briefed that I couldn't even use any of the photos. And I've spent more than I'd like to think about on marketing and advertisements that generated zero return on investment.

Every time I've 'lost' money in business, I've had two choices:

Option A. Feel sorry for myself about making a 'wrong' decision, let my ego take over and feel embarrassed and even bitter toward the other person or situation.

I think by now, you know I'm not the type of person to sit at home all day worrying about the money I lost, ruminating on 'what could have been', berating myself and feeling anxious and embarrassed that I made a bad investment decision.

Of course, I'm going to think about what went wrong and how to make better decisions next time. But I'm not going to beat myself up, thinking:

- That's a lot of money to lose.
- All my hard work is down the drain.
- I should have known better.

That shit is DRAIN-ING. And we don't do draining. That's why I prefer Option B.

> **Option B.** Understand that money is unlimited in this world – and it flows in and out.

Sure, I allow myself to feel a little disappointed. But I cut my losses quickly and I don't attach energy to it and move on. I proceed as usual and stay grounded in knowing that 'what you focus on expands'. I chose to concentrate on the fact that money is all energy. It flows in and out so I can focus on growth, opportunities and moving forward, and I know that money will flow back to me.

Here's an example of one of the many times I received less than anticipated. I decided to invest in a brand designer. I was so excited to step into the next elevation of my brand; I felt ready to be *seen* and step into my authority in a bigger way.

Now, I could have designed my branding, website and graphics, but I knew my time and energy would be better spent elsewhere. I found an amazing designer who had worked with some very high-profile clients. At the time, my logical brain said this was the right next step, so I signed up and set to work ready to level up.

I completed a lengthy 50-page questionnaire and in hindsight this was the first tiny red flag that maybe we weren't on the same page. But I trusted the process and completed it. After a week, they sent over the first brand concept. When I tell you it looked like a promotion for *The Bold and the Beautiful* from 1996, I am not kidding. It was not my vision, it did not buy into my goals, and didn't showcase my brand the way I wanted it to.

I gave them the benefit of the doubt and asked them to revise it. This time, I opened the email to see a creative edit on all my images, complete with a glitter effect on my clothing. It gave Myspace circa 2008 vibes and was certainly not what I was going for again. From here, I spent over ten hours on phone calls, sending concepts and directing them on the design to finally receive the third iteration, which you can probably guess by now was way off base. Honestly, it couldn't get much worse. I had handed them my vision on a silver platter but no matter how much I communicated; it wasn't getting any better.

I decided at that moment to be honest with them and part ways. I had already paid for the work they had completed to that point, and they refused a refund (tip: always ask for what you want, it's worth a try), so I cut my losses and moved on.

I 'lost' thousands of dollars with that little (read: very long) exercise plus the time that I had wasted overseeing the project.

This wasn't the first time, and it won't be the last time I'm going to lose in business. The upside is that I really connected with my brand and well and truly recognised what I did not want it to represent.

So, I don't dwell on the loss. I know that my energy is better spent on creating *more* income and wealth and focusing on the outcomes I CAN control. I have and always will choose Option B because I know where I am going and what I am capable of!

Now, by choosing Option B it doesn't mean you just let money fly out of your pocket as if it means nothing. You're a badass business owner, so holding high standards, expectations and boundaries around your business is key. However, when things are out of your control and you have invested all the energy that you can into the situation, letting go is the only way to move forward.

Does it hurt a little to see the money evaporate? Heck yes! But it's how fast you move through that feeling and what you decide to do with the lesson that is the key to your success.

I think we can all agree that Option A, feeling sorry for ourselves, embarrassed and/or bitter would not provide a path toward your goals. If you choose to stay and sit in Option A you are going to stay 'stuck', it's slowing you down. It's taking up energy that you could be directing elsewhere. And it just downright feels horrible.

I will *always* choose to operate from a place of abundance and opportunity, not scarcity and fear. There are so many paths to success, but I can guarantee it feels a whole lot easier when you get out of your own way and work on yourself first.

You need to fail more to succeed more

A powerful way to look at failure is that it is proof that you're out there trying new strategies, getting out of your comfort zone and taking big leaps toward your success.

I get excited when my intended power plans go wrong or I'm challenged to think smarter because it's a reminder that I'm changing things up, doing things I haven't done before and that's the path to growth, baby!

I would rather fall on my face and skin my knees than never have tried or never have aimed high. So, if success is what you want, you need to come to terms with the fact you're going to 'fail' a whole lot more along the way.

The road to success is not LOGICAL at all. And that's why those who are adaptable, willing to try something new and aren't afraid to 'fail' will continue to create more success than those who aren't. Period.

One Person's 'Failure' is Another's Success

We've already touched on the point that success looks different to everyone, and failure does too.

When I decided to exit my various companies, people also asked me if it felt like I'd failed. I've started five different businesses and I've had people who don't know all the details say to me, 'Ahh they must have all been failures then, or you'd still be doing them, right?'

At first, I was taken aback. I would credit exiting and selling my businesses, as some of my biggest business successes. They were profitable when I ran them, and I made big profits when I sold them. It's interesting to me that other people look at it as one big flop, simply because I exited, but that's their limitations

– a reflection of their inner thoughts and beliefs, rather than a truth.

Sure, my vision changed along the way. At one stage, running and growing those businesses was my ultimate Fantasy Land goal. But our vision can change. I could have held on tight to that idea and pushed through my burnout to look 'successful' to others watching on. But the reality was, that my success compass had changed direction – and along with it my goals and vision had been realigned.

At first, I thought that success meant completing every strategy, reaching every goal and doing all of them at once. Working 24/7 in the pursuit of feeling and looking successful on paper felt right at the time and profit was king. For instance, my events and photoshoot venue were wildly successful: that business was profitable, successful and easy to operate. Why would anyone walk away from that?

Yes, it was constantly booked out. And yes, it was turning a good profit. But I had to drive 40 minutes there and home every day to let clients in and show prospective bookings through the venue, and I hated the rigidity of having to be stuck in an office.

My idea of 'success' changed. At the core of my values is being challenged and having growth and adventure, but success to me also looks like flexibility, ease and freedom. Running this business was causing me stress and anxiety. It was telling me (actually, it was screaming at me) that this was not my version of success anymore. This was no longer what I wanted in my future. This is not where I am going. And so, I exited that business. That was the easiest decision I've ever made, and it helped me realise something huge for me (and my clients) in business:

You. Are. Allowed. To. Change. Your. Mind.

You can reimagine what success looks like for you at any time; that's the beauty of being your own boss. Success and failure are not binary – they're not defined, written in stone and unchangeable. And when you understand that you are in control of your own life and success, it all changes. You can choose what path you take. It may not always be easy, but it's a choice.

It's okay to realise that *this is not what I really want*. You can let go of the initial goal, head back to the drawing board and go after a different goal. You might be thinking that letting go sounds like a failure, because that's what we've been taught and told to believe, right? If you retreat, back up, give up – it's a failure. But this isn't true. Changing your mind doesn't make you a failure (read that again). Whether you ultimately decide to push forward and make your goals happen, or you feel called to choose safety and comfort, neither of these decisions is wrong or right.

It all comes back to what *you* value. If your highest value is security and comfort, then retreating is not a failure at all. In that case, it is a success! For me, my biggest values have always been growth and adventure, so I will set out to create a way to make my Fantasy Land goals happen. I will not give up. I will persevere. I will make that shit happen. But I also reserve the right to change my mind (I'm looking at you, photo studio). And guess what? That doesn't mean anything. Remember, failure is the meaning that you apply to situations. The situation is you made a choice. That. Is. It.

It doesn't mean success. It doesn't mean failure. It's all a matter of PERSPECTIVE. If your goals are misaligned with what you value, then it's just a redirection, right? When you understand that YOU are in control of your own life, your whole reality changes.

Key Insights

- Look at 'failure' as just another step in the process to success; it's merely a circumstance and an opportunity to overcome a new challenge.

- When you face a challenge or feel like you've failed, separate the facts from the stories or meanings you've created about it. When you stick to the facts, you can find the ways forward.

- There are going to be times when things don't go as planned in business (and life), but without some level of risk, there can't be reward – it's simply how you GROW.

- When you understand that YOU are in CONTROL of your own life, your whole reality changes.

- The only time you can truly fail is if you fail to learn the lessons. The quicker you learn the lesson, the faster you can move back to ACTION.

Remember: you're not here to play small. You're not here to make others feel more comfortable by keeping yourself down. You're here to play BIG. Because when you do this, you become MAGNETIC.

CHAPTER 9

Your Limitless Self

This is what you're here for; now you get to create your new identity and step into becoming truly limitless!

I've mentored clients who spent all their time and energy working on their marketing and messaging as they strive to position themselves as a 'leader' or 'game changer' or 'insert other characteristics here'. But if *you* don't see yourself as a leader or game changer or whatever characteristic you're going for, no amount of marketing is going to change that.

Sure, good marketing initially attracts some clients, but then what happens:

- If you genuinely, wholeheartedly, do not believe you have what it takes to make an impact?
- If you let imposter syndrome creep its way in?
- If you spend too much time watching what other people are doing rather than focusing your energy on what you CAN control.

How can you really step into your true power?

You need to step into *becoming* that leader first. Because

once you become the leader you know you can be, and shift your identity, behaviour and thoughts, then *of course* your marketing will position you as a leader because it's just *who you are*.

When I launched my first business, despite being confident of what I could achieve, I didn't want to be 'seen'. For instance, the 'about me' section on my website simply listed my name as 'Jess' (no surname and no way to Google more information about me); I didn't have any photos; my brand had no visible founder, and that was the way I presented it.

These were all subconscious decisions to keep me safe from judgment and prevent myself from having to completely own my power. Then, when I started building a personal brand and gaining some recognition, I slowly started to reveal more about myself. But I was *still* watering myself down. I would over-edit every single piece of content so it didn't offend anyone, ensuring that my opinions and decisions wouldn't be misunderstood. I wanted to be a leader, an inspiration, and a motivating force – but my intentions and my actions weren't aligned, as I was still in 'people pleaser' mode: Jess, The Nice Girl.

For instance, whenever someone questioned my pricing or offers, I threw my standards and boundaries out the window and instantly agreed to their requests. When working with clients, I bent over backwards to be accommodating and I tried to mould myself to fit other's needs, schedules, and demands.

I fell into the trap of comparison when I saw others online being super successful and magnetic, and I thought I needed to be more like them. In fact, to be successful, I thought I needed to be more bubbly, loving and fun, louder, sweeter and NICER!

It's easy to fall into the trap of being oblivious to your worth because you're waiting for external validation or you desperately want to be appreciated by others, instead of owning your power and seeing it within yourself.

I wasn't being seen as the authority I knew I was and could be because I wasn't able to hold that energy. Underneath it all was my need to be liked. Subconsciously, I was manipulating situations to feel that sense of validation. I wanted to attract higher-level clients and opportunities that matched what I knew I was capable of – but having the inner belief was just one piece of the puzzle. It required me to step into that identity and be able to hold it.

Yet, if you'd asked me at the time, I would've said I already completely owned who I was. I'd already built a massive personal brand, despite all those subconscious beliefs that were holding me back. Once I became aware of my limiting beliefs (using the shadows tools in Chapter 4) and started to shift my habits, show up and be more visible, I started receiving DMs with people writing 'I don't know what you're doing but keep it up!' and 'I love your no-bullshit vibe lately!'

And what was more belief-affirming was that higher-level clients began reaching out to work with me like crazy. My business grew and I hit record revenue months. Funny how that happens when you work on yourself while taking action. It was no accident. It was super intentional using the deeper subconscious work I was doing for myself.

I encourage you to use the strategies I've discussed in previous chapters to identify your patterns and dig into your shadows and limiting beliefs to discover the underlying mindset blocks that hold you back. Seek out the blocks, work through them and tap into your highest-level self. This is who you are at your core: the foundation of your limitless self.

You already have everything within you to SUCCEED.

You just need to give yourself permission to take the leap, to commit to your goals and dreams, and then get out of your own damn way.

Creating the Limitless You

Right now, every single thing in your reality is a result of the decisions you have made ... E V E R Y T H I N G ... And what influences those decisions are intrinsic to how you see yourself.

Let's take a moment to think about it like this ... if you tell yourself that you're bad with numbers and that you've never been good at math, then you aren't likely to choose engineering as your university degree, are you? If you believe you're unfit and someone asks you to join them in a 10km fun run, what do you think you're going to say? And if you view yourself as being terrible with money, what decision do you think you are going to make when it comes to wanting to start a business and investing in yourself?

On the flip side, if you view yourself as a high achiever, who always finds a way to get what you want and will persevere until it happens – what do you think you're going to do when someone tells you it can't be done? Or says, 'no' straight to your face? You're going to continue to persevere and find a way to make it happen, that's what.

In other words, to step into creating limitless success – it makes sense that you first need to become limitless. Okay, so how do you do that exactly? It starts with the understanding that the person you are today and *every single part* of your identity – the way you dress, the way you talk, how you lead yourself, and the hobbies and interests you have – is created and crafted over time. But you have the power to change it.

This is not about changing yourself or looking for elements of your identity that you believe are wrong, the intent is not to become someone else. Instead, you step into your highest self and shine light on the parts of you that haven't been unlocked yet. It is about becoming *more of you*.

To change your perception of who you are and the results you could create, you need to see yourself *right now*. If you don't have visibility on how you see yourself, you don't have the power to change, influence or control the outcomes. And we want to be the ones in control around here. Otherwise, it's like trying to type a destination into your maps app without entering the current location; it cannot possibly create a route to get you there without the starting point.

Everything you believe you are – or you are not – makes up your concept of self.

If you don't know what you're capable of, worthy of, or how you view yourself, how do you even begin to take control and create your reality? It's easy to continue to cruise through life on autopilot – but the magic happens when you bring awareness to yourself because it's only then you can change.

Without reevaluating your concept of self and updating it to reflect how you want to play in the world, the same old 'you' will continue to show up. Again, I'm not saying who you are right now isn't 'enough'; I'm saying that everyone needs to grow, change, and evolve, rather than settling for what we have now.

Say, for example, you think of yourself as a risk-averse person, but you want to start a business and grow it at lightning speed. That's going to take some risks, and definitely some big ones. You will need to pull up those big girl pants, avoid negative self-talk and be prepared to go big.

Get to know your current self

The first step to shifting your concept of self and stepping into your limitless next level identity is to understand how you see yourself right now – this is a great little exercise that helps:

In your journal, describe yourself in five words: What kind of person are you? Don't overthink it, just literally write the first five words that emerge before your conscious mind has time to think. Here are some prompts:

- I am
- I do
- I am good at
- I am capable of
- I thrive when I
- I am not
- I don't do
- I am not good at
- I am not capable of ...

None of the words that come to mind in this exercise are right or wrong and they might also contradict each other. It might be that you feel you are ambitious but also disorganised. Empathetic and opinionated. Confident, but also insecure.

Ask yourself:

Who do I need to become, to see myself, to be truly LIMITLESS?

What words describe the person you need to be to reach your Fantasy Land goals?

What traits do you need to bring more into consciousness and what do you need to detach from and let go?

If you see yourself as a badass with strong boundaries and high standards, how would you show up in your business?

The words you write down can help you identify the gaps between your current self and limitless self – the areas of yourself that you can develop further so you can achieve those Fantasy Land goals.

I previously labelled myself as an introvert, someone shy and quiet. If I'd completed this exercise before I stepped into my big Fantasy goals, those are the words I would have written on the page. Being introverted was a *huge* part of who I was. I created marketing content and was even considering writing a book about being a quiet but successful introvert (but this book is way better) – it was an integral part of my identity, and it served me for a time.

However, as I grew and evolved, I no longer identified with the introverted Jess, I'd done the work and developed my new intentions, values and goals. The label 'introverted' no longer served me in the way that it once did. If I thought of myself as an introvert now, I would feel capped – I would use it as an excuse to water myself down, not share my bold opinions and continue to fly under the radar.

By nature, I do love my alone time to recharge and I'm not the loudest person in the room, but that doesn't mean I'm not confident or bold. Don't tell yourself stories that limit who you can be, how you can show up in the world and what you can achieve. There is *no limit* to your Fantasy Land goals! The question for you is, how high are you willing to aim?

Hello, Ego

Ego, particularly a strong well-developed ego, gets a bad rap. But the truth is, we all have one, and as you lean into this process of becoming The New You, you need to understand that ego is not a dirty word.

Despite what you've learnt or read or been told over the years – having an ego is a good thing. Your ego is your sense of personal identity and concept of self. Without an ego, you wouldn't be able to have any relationships or goals – you'd be a helpless creature with no idea of who you are or what you value.

Your ego is a blank piece of paper and, over time, you add to the list of who you want to be and you pull in aspects of your identity based on who you consciously think you should be. Your ego is formed through life experiences that mould you into the person you choose. Ego is *not* something bad to avoid (you can't avoid it anyway). Instead, you need to use it to your advantage.

Your brain is so bloody clever that it can filter out certain memories or details, just so it can uphold your concept of self. Anything outside of confirmed thoughts, beliefs and behaviours will be rejected. And on the flip side, it will also seek out and remember moments where your concept of self is confirmed. It's like a lawyer pulling together all the evidence to prove their case simply because she's been hired, regardless of the actual truth or facts.

Our ego is the key to shifting our identity to a deeper level, where we truly live and breathe it. It's all well and good to try and tell yourself that you're a leader, that you're successful in business and that you're making an impact in this world. But until those traits are truly a part of who you are, and they influence how you show up each day, your ego will continue to ignore all the proof that supports your vision.

For example, if you genuinely don't believe you are an engaging public speaker, it doesn't matter if ten people tell you every day that you are a gun presenter: your mind will simply ignore all this positive encouragement. To step into your next level identity and become a confident public speaker, you need to be very conscious and attentive to find the proof of where you are showing up as a leader, or already serving as your highest self.

This means a combination of finding the evidence in your life where you already show these certain traits and create new evidence by taking action. This could include:

- 'Going live' on social media.
- Proactively reaching out to be a guest on other people's podcasts.
- Saying yes to small in-person speaking opportunities.
- Offering to facilitate meetings.

Over time, leaning into public speaking will become more subconscious.

Showing up as that confident, capable version of 'you' will become second nature. And before you know it, you'll be as comfortable on stage, commanding a crowd of 50,000 and channelling your version of Beyonce!

Finding the evidence and proof of your limitless self

First, we need to find all the evidence that you are already showing up as your limitless self. Reflect on past moments or experiences, how you navigated certain challenges, or the action you have taken toward your goals and journal on these questions:

What is the evidence that I am showing up as my next-level limitless self?

Gather evidence that shows you're on the right track: new clients, bigger opportunities, shifting mindsets and alignments. It may be through past moments or experiences, how you navigated certain challenges, or the action you have already taken toward your goals. Remember to write it down. The more often you write it down, the more evidence your subconscious has toward truly embodying your limitless self.

How can I embody my highest-level self each day?

The second part of becoming your limitless self is taking action in alignment with your highest self. What behaviour am I showing up with? How do I see myself each day? What things am I doing and what actions am I taking? What actions can I take today, that allow me to show up as my limitless self? As you embody these traits, the more undeniable proof your subconscious has to update your identity at the core.

When It's Time to Let Go

Before you start on your new journey, you need to let go of the habits, behaviours and blocks that no longer serve you. I'm sorry (not sorry), it's time to leave all that baggage behind – these are *not* coming with you to that next level!

When we have Fantasy Land level visions, often they require us to let go of our past selves and current situations that won't serve us at the next level. I'm not going to lie – this can be hard as Teresa discovered. This is her story:

> When my client Teresa, a successful brand and website designer, wanted to go to the next level she made some very big decisions about what to keep and what to let go to attain those big Fantasy Land goals.
>
> Teresa came to me feeling unfulfilled in her business, while she had great clients and was making a decent income, the work she was doing was no longer lighting her up. When she discovered her new passion for Human Design, she felt pulled toward creating business services that were purely around her new interests. She knew things had to change to make space for these new and exciting offers.
>
> Teresa looked at her current business and made the hard decision to let go of very profitable clients that bought in over 90% of her revenue in pursuit of her next level, which was far more aligned with who she knew she was here to be. This required such a deep level of self-trust and belief on Teresa's part: it was a process of letting go of people and income.
>
> It paid off, and Teresa is now thriving. She's replaced the income from those 'lost' clients and she elevated her standards for the people who get to be in her energy and who she works with.

But taking that first step? That wasn't easy. It may not be easy for you, either. Letting go of the habits, behaviours, parts of your business and blocks that no longer serve you is crucial – you need to operate at the next level so that people can see your limitless self. It's only then that you're going to attract those next level clients and opportunities.

This is the OPPOSITE of what I see a lot of people with big visions do. They don't let go – instead, they want to hold onto things until they reach a certain milestone. They want proof that the next level is coming *before* they let the current situation go. And so, I hear comments like:

- I'll stop doing that *when* I get to
- I'll close that part of my business *when* I
- I'll let go of those clients *after* I
- I'll get rid of that staff member *once* I …

I don't believe success is by accident at all. If you really want to fast-track success, just as my client Teresa did, it requires a huge level of deep self-trust – and you need to be prepared to jump before you feel ready.

I have seen and experienced first-hand how holding onto past identities, parts of your business, behaviours and decisions that may serve you now but won't serve you in the future, will hold you back from making progress toward your version of unstoppable success.

The alternative? You need to operate as Future You, not NOW you. For instance: Future You wants to be a brand or name to watch in your industry, to be quoted in the media, to be invited to speak or showcase at industry events. Future You wants to be winning awards in your business category.

Take a moment to imagine what Future You looks like. What are you doing? Or maybe, it's what you're not doing? If that's who you want to be, then you need to step into that energy *now*. You don't wait until X, Y and Z happen – you start today.

Think about it like this. You are holding a handful of balloons. You can see all your Fantasy Land level goals right there in the clouds above. You are so ready to hit those big fluffy clouds and the balloons are ready to take you there. You look down and you have these heavy, unwieldy weights holding you down. The weights are keeping you safe on the ground (that's good right?); they provide a real sense of comfort.

No matter how badly you want to, you're not going to go *anywhere* without first letting go of those weights.

What most people do is look up at those clouds bursting with Fantasy Land goals and they plan and they work and they dream about taking that journey, but they don't release a single weight.

They might even add MORE weights to their balloons. More low profit offers, more ill-fitting clients and more work that keeps them busy, but doesn't fulfil or propel them towards their next big goals. Imagine how fast you would reach your goals and step into becoming your limitless self if you remove these weights. With less resistance it's going to be a whole lot faster to become Future You.

This process of letting go is something I've been through myself several times, most recently in my coaching business when I took a serious look at how I was working. I did an audit of my business and asked myself: 'If I want to level up, what are the things I need to let go of? What are all the things that are working for me and all the things that are not?'

At the time, a big part of my business was my first membership program. I loved delivering the lessons in that program and I enjoyed the opportunity to guide so many smart, switched-on women towards becoming the very best versions of themselves. However, when I looked ahead at my big vision for the future, I knew this program wasn't going to be an integral part of my business model – or in fact, part of my ideal business at all.

Once I'd created that next level vision, I saw a whole new business model emerge. As a result, I decided to close my membership program.

Let's be clear: It was *hard*. My membership program wasn't just profitable, it was successful and growing. It didn't take up much of my time and I could have easily kept it ticking over. As far as weights go, these were light as a feather. The decision to close it was a choice to turn the tap off on an ongoing, consistent and regular income stream. It would have been all too easy to simply keep running my membership program and enjoy the safety of a regular income, while also striving for my bigger picture goals.

But I knew deep down it was holding me back. My messaging and price point weren't right for where I was going. I had outgrown the lessons I was sharing in my sessions, as you do when you are committed to evolving. I just knew that the act of letting go would create the space to manifest and step into the next version of my big Fantasy Land goals.

Sometimes you just have to say: 'Actually, I am going to let go of this big chunk of income and I am not going to let it put me into a scarcity mindset.' I trusted – heck, I KNEW – that the moves I was making were going to create that next-level success for me. Spoiler alert: they did!

I went from clients paying $50 per month for my membership, to dream clients entering my world within a few months and paying me $56,000 – upfront. In the interests of full disclosure, I did have other offers priced at around $9000 at the time, but needless to say, it was a massive jump from working with a large member base to focusing on a selection of VIP clients and enjoying a massive shift in income.

Some might say there was some risk in my decision to shut off an income stream, but I didn't see it as risky. If anything, it would have been riskier to stay rooted in my old way of doing things, earning the same old money, repeating the same old offers and achieving the same old results. That not only sounded like a ticket to Boring Town, but it completely lacked any growth, which is an important value to me.

Over to you: let's say your next level of success was guaranteed. Let's assume you're making $10,000 per month right now and you're guaranteed to hit your new goal of making $100,000 per month or even well above that.

If this is a *fact*; if your next income level is *guaranteed*; and if you are making decisions and plotting your next moves as if this new income and next level of success is *100% locked in*, it's time to begin to let go of the behaviours and limiting parts of your identity that don't serve you at this next level. The parts that play small, that operate from a place of fear and scarcity and hold you back. You need to update and let go of these parts of yourself to become your next level self. This can mean making some tough decisions – but it's all necessary for your growth.

For instance, when I was leaning into updating my identity to be in alignment with my highest self, I didn't just let go of my membership program. I also let go of my people pleasing, my desire to always be liked and any tendency I had towards discounting or undervaluing my products. I stopped watering myself down in my marketing so as not to offend anyone and I stopped saying yes to meetings at times that were not suitable for me. Overall, I stopped running my business for everyone else's happiness but mine.

I stepped into my leadership era and started to truly see myself as the successful unstoppable badass entrepreneur that I had become. I had high standards and was unapologetic about it. And I was only just getting started!

The bottom line for you? To get to the next level of where *you're* going, it's important that you release anything that isn't going to elevate you. You're going to need to clean some energetic leaks up, so you can make space to call in the next level.

—— 💡 ——

It's time to let go

To take the next step in your evolution and let go of those identities, behaviours, and ways of doing business that no longer serve you, ask yourself:

What behaviours and limiting parts of my identity do I need to let go of?

What offers, services, and products do I need to remove?

Would I still do things the way I'm doing them now?

Would I still work with the same clients?

Charge the same prices? Have the same support team? Employ the same staff? Entertain the same requests? Work towards the same goals?

> Make a big list of things that are not coming with you at the next level. It may be hard to let go but think of that badass limitless self and do it for her.

———————

Remember: you're not here to play small anymore. You're not here to make others feel more comfortable just by keeping yourself down. You're here to play BIG. Because when you can do this, you become MAGNETIC.

I've already touched on this a few times, but it's important, I need you to really 'get it': to step into who you are in the future, you need to embrace your limitless self and make it happen now. Before you're ready. Before the moons have aligned and all your ducks are in a row. Before the perfect conditions have arrived.

Do it now.

Instead of waiting until your external world changes, change who you are first. Act as if you're at the pinnacle of your success already.

Once you know it, believe and live it, then your external world changes to meet your inner world ... and that's when limitless opportunities begin showing up. You're in the energy of truly owning your power, which makes it effortless to attract more of everything you desire.

Key Insights

- Before you can change your perception of who you are (which is how you get the result you want) – you first need to understand how you see yourself *right now*.

- Look deep and discover the underlying mindset blocks that are holding you back.

- Ego is *not* something to avoid – you can't avoid it anyway. Instead, you need to use it to your advantage.

- To get to the next level 'limitless you', you're going to need to let go of parts of your business, limiting beliefs and identity traits that no longer serve you (and probably before you feel ready to).

- You already have everything within you to SUCCEED.

Whatever your goals are right now,
I urge you to take it one step further –
dream a LOT bigger. If this excites you,
GREAT. If it scares you, EVEN BETTER!

Today is the start of the rest of your life. You're in the driver's seat. YOU get to decide what you do next.

CHAPTER 10

It's Time

You didn't make it to the final pages of this book because you didn't want to make a change. Because you're happy with what you've achieved so far. Because you want to stay where you are right now.

I *know* you're ready to make a change. So, if you were looking for a sign to shake things up and step into that person you know you can be – THIS IS IT. You already know you're capable of making insane wild success (more than you already have), and sometimes it's our true potential that scares us the most!

And yes, I know you are out there making big moves already. But I can also guarantee there is at least one goal you haven't acted towards yet: a big, audacious, crazy, next level idea and opportunity that you are sitting on (you know what I'm talking about).

The more you sit on your potential, knowing that if you do, in fact, take the leap, you'd probably achieve your goal – makes you less likely to take that leap. Our egos get a fun little boost by sitting in that 'potential' and we feel as though we have already achieved it. You get to enjoy the *idea* of achieving it without any of the risk, challenges or doing the damn thing – but I know you didn't come here to just sit on that potential.

If you want to take it from 'potential' to 'achieving', you need to take ACTION – the kind that scares you a little.

There's never going to be a 'perfect' time to step into your next level. The one you already know you're more than capable of. And there's no point waiting *until* you have enough time, or money, or experience, or clients, or confidence, or [insert what you're waiting for here] to take that leap. Because you're never going to be 'ready' – it just doesn't exist.

I know you have big ideas, big plans, big wants and big visions inside you. I know that you have Fantasy Land level goals you want to achieve and I'm so excited that by reading this book, you're trusting me to help you take the next step on your journey. Here's the thing … today is the start of the rest of your life. You're in the driver's seat here. YOU get to decide what you do next. Life doesn't happen *to* you, you are the one in control, so are you ready to dial it up a notch? Heck yeah, you are! (If you said no then I'd go back and re-read this entire book! But since you've made it this far, I already know you're ready.)

So, what comes next? You need to go deep and do the inner work that's essential to shake off any of those subconscious limiting beliefs, then get out of your own way and take BOLD action.

Yes, you're going to have to 'jump' before you're ready.

You need to step – actually, LEAP – outside of your comfort zone, and it probably won't feel great at first. It might feel uncomfortable, unfamiliar, or even downright painful to let go. But what I can promise you is that you already have the ability to create massive success within you. It's right there, waiting to be uncovered.

I'm not saying that this is going to be easy, it's not always going to be a walk in the park. But what's on the other side is the life and business of your wildest dreams, and it's undeniably worth it. It is possible to achieve crazy levels of success and do so without sacrificing your health, relationships and all the other things that you value. You can achieve more, without working more, because increased success doesn't equal increased work. I know that as fact because I'm living proof.

People are going to say, 'no' and some might even think you're crazy or a little delusional. You're going to fall (and probably cry at some point too), but if you continue to get back up, if you continue to 'find another way', you're going to get where you want to go, hit those goals, and achieve the unstoppable success you deserve, that I know for sure.

The only real 'failure' is the one that takes place when you fail to learn the lesson, so pay attention to the challenges that come your way and use them to level up.

No more waiting, okay?
This is your moment.
Don't wait for Monday.
Don't wait for next week.
And don't you dare wait until next year!

Start making moves today as if the results you dream of are already guaranteed!

My clients often joke with me in those moments they hear

my voice in their head pushing them off the metaphorical cliff: 'Just do it ... now!' If you find yourself playing smaller, self-sabotaging or dulling down your goals, try this: imagine me in your head (in a non-creepy way), with all the wisdom I've shared with you from this book, cheering you on from the sidelines, with a loving kick up the butt. I'm right here with you every step of the way.

So now, take your big, bold goals and push them even further to unstoppable success. Dream a whole lot bigger, bolder and crazier. What you can achieve is truly limitless because if there's a will, there's ALWAYS a way!

Repeat after me: 'Just watch me!'

It is possible to achieve crazy levels of success and do so without sacrificing your health, relationships and all the other things that you value. Increased success doesn't equal increased work. I know that as fact because I'm living proof.

About the Author
Jessica Williamson

A dynamic serial entrepreneur driven by a no-nonsense attitude and a passion for challenging the status quo. She's an award winning Mindset & Business Mentor to thousands of women, TedX speaker, author and host of the top global ranking Podcast, Jess Williamson the Podcast.

Jess made headlines in 2016 after founding her first venture, a swimwear brand, that showcased at New York Fashion Week just one week after launching online. Since then Jess has scaled five businesses by age 25 and created unstoppable success.

The journey for Jess certainly wasn't smooth sailing. Running all 5 businesses at once in 2019, Jess became very familiar with burnout, adrenal fatigue in the pursuit of building her businesses. Throughout this journey Jess learnt how to define her version of success, sold 3 of the businesses and continues to bend reality when it comes to 'illogical success' and playing in Fantasy Land.

Never one to shy away from leaping head first into any goal, she's committed to empowering women and proving that achieving unconventional success is entirely possible with a whole lot of audacity, self-belief and business strategy to back you.